AF682825

FOREWORD

There is little doubt the City of North Bay would be a very different place today were it not for the continuous activity of the North Bay Board of Trade / District Chamber of Commerce. The Board / Chamber and the community have grown together during the past 100 years.

To tell the story of the Board / Chamber is to relate the story of the commercial, industrial and professional development of the city. There is no one organization of citizens which has played a more important role than the Board / Chamber.

On October 19, 1894, a handful of merchants and professionals in North Bay banded together to form the Board of Trade, dedicated to community service. Through the years they did their job with devotion, serving many fields of work including, municipal administration, on boards and commissions and in fraternal and welfare organizations. Their voice has been a strong one, whether it spoke locally or through higher levels of provincial or federal interest. Individual members have sponsored many sports teams from youth to adult. Many teams have achieved honors outside the community and without financial support would not have had the opportunity to compete. Collectively the Board / Chamber has organized many community events that have provided entertainment, promoted culture and enriched our lives.

'Boosting The Bay' is a commemorative book for the resident, visitor or student who wishes to learn a little more about the heritage of North Bay seen through the eyes of an active organization. North Bay wasn't built in a day and has had its fair share of prosperity and lean times. The Board / Chamber certainly doesn't take credit for all the developments you will read about. It has in concert with other levels of government and other groups worked towards the betterment of the community. Because it is a large organization with a working, democratic constitution decisions and stances made have been well thought out and representative of community interests. You will gain an appreciation for the role this organization has played in the city's evolution.

'Boosting The Bay' is a story about our heritage and how the North Bay Board of Trade / District Chamber of Commerce helped develop our community. It is written in an easy-to-read and understandable format. It is not an in-depth history book that is about to prove a theory or point of view, it is a book that reflects upon the people who lived and worked in North Bay. Their contributions comprise the changing fabric of any community.

I have tried to bring life to our heritage. Pointing to people, landmarks and developments will help the reader in piecing together the factors and events that comprise our collective history. The record left by the Board / Chamber is an invaluable source for studying our community development.

'Boosting the Bay' is a collection of short stories and photographs that occur in chronological order. It looks at its location before the time the first white explorers acknowledged North Bay's important geographical location. The proposed Canadian Pacific Railroad plays a significant part in the initiation of North Bay and of its founder - John Ferguson. Location and a sense of timing are important factors in the town's early development.

The formation of the Board of Trade in 1894 is a significant event and lays the foundation for important developments during the following 100 years. The Board / Chamber has played a key role promoting growth strategies and in campaigning for improved urban services. It includes the changing of the name to the North Bay Chamber of Commerce in 1948, a trend of modernization throughout the country. Within this book Board is used for the period, 1894-1948, while Chamber is used for the period 1949-1994 ("District" was added in 1955).

Originally the Board was the bringing

together of businessmen who needed a meeting place to conduct trade, it evolved into an organization whose primary mandate was a concern with the well being of the community as a whole. Within the organization committees were formed, responsible for a varity of commercial and community interests, and these interests have changed with the changing times.

Members have actively participated on many committees and in earlier times took up leadership positions on municipal council. They always kept the viewpoints of the private sector in the forefront of community development. Perhaps the most significant achievement of the Board / Chamber has been its ability to attract to community service so many dedicated and capable people. Their continuous and volunteer efforts have made our community a better place to live. Remembering its worthy people is to acknowledge the soul of the city.

W.P. (Bill) Steer

ACKNOWLEDGEMENTS

'riting local history is that it is all wrapped up within a cloak of unique people

t other places in Northern Ontario - is a community where the collective will n government or industry, attempted to direct and foster its growth.

'hat I am indebted in helping to bring this book together. As very little of preserved in written form we asked the community to bring in their ıy.

ıt and these arrived at our Chamber in the form of photographs and written 'eciated and are found throughout the book. Credits are affixed to their

of photographs is the North Bay Area Museum Archives. Reg Tremblay the author to arrange the wide range of photographs in this book, most of before by the public. It is hoped the museum will soon start construction at Lee Park.

itten entirely on the history of North Bay. But copies of Anson Gard's, 'The 909; W.K.P. Kennedy's, 'North Bay,'1961; Hartley Trussler's, 'The Best of Bay,' 1982 and Michael Barnes', 'Gateway City,' 1982 were invaluable

formation on specific topics then the microfilm of the North Bay Public is the place to visit. The collection of North Bay Nugget articles going only sources of information available to the researcher. Newspapers are own right and our local publication marked its 50th anniversary as a brary also has an extensive North Bay File, full of interesting readings. ce is the collection of memorabilia available at the Nipissing University ary.

t resources to any writer is the living testimony of people who have "lived in being able to research a little more than 50 years of the Chamber as managers of the organization. These are Bruce McLeod, 1944-1956, our present manager, Glen DeVuono, 1966 to present. These gentlemen hecking out people and places, events and happenings. In particular, author and the product. The Chamber is proud to have them in their them for their assistance.

As a member of the Chamber (North Bay Public Library), Paul Walker took on the task of spearheading this book project to help commemorate the Chamber's centennial. I thank him for believing in the project and the support he has lent to making it a reality.

Editing is the final stage of the writing process and writers rely on others to polish up the final product. I thank Joanne Landriault, Hazel Swindle, Paul Walker, Glen DeVuono, Heather Atkins and Carrie Pinkerton-Steer for their many hours of critique that lead to more refinement - "making it right."

I am grateful to family and friends, and especially my wife, Carrie, who have lent their support, encouragement and enthusiasm; also to The Nipissing Board of Education, who has supported me in my writing endeavours.

We must salute the North Bay Board of Trade / District Chamber of Commerce because it has provided 100 years of community service. Its continuing leadership has made North Bay a better place - in so many ways.

And to all those who lived and live in North Bay, from pioneers to present residents; only by living here can you appreciate what we have to share and care about.

Wilston Steer

CONTENTS

"Boosterism"

An explanation of the the growth of North Bay must contain an examination of many variables.

Factors include changing trends in regional, national and international development. Also, of importance are changes in agriculture, transportation, and industrial technology; migration patterns and the role of individuals and groups within the community.

One must examine all factors, and within specific periods the growth rate may be the result of only a few predominant ones. In other words a sense of time and place plays a crucial role in the explanation of how and why North Bay came into being and flourished as one of the few cities in the northland.

In the mid 1800's New Ontario was part of Ontario, a vast and uninhabited land, it had no urban centres. Except for the remaining Hudson Bay Company posts and some small mining starts along the shores of Lake Huron and Lake Superior there was no commercial development. The population in North Bay was completely transitory. Lumbermen, prospectors and trappers were seasonal residents.

By the 1880's some early pioneers had reached the South River and had established the village of Nipissing. Mattawa was booming and was the most northern community along the Ottawa Valley. Settlers were moving towards what would become Rutherglen and Bonfield. But North Bay was not even an idea in anyone's mind. In fact what we know as the downtown area was a land of exposed bedrock and ponds with little soil or agricultural promise.

Only the skill and initiative of individuals and groups would translate opportunity into reality. One such group that played an important role in the early development of our community was the Board of Trade, later to become the Chamber of Commerce (1948).

Organizations of merchants and craftsmen have been around for centuries going back to the guilds formed in the Middle Ages. Their power influenced working and trading conditions. The guilds in some repects were the forerunners of trade associations and trade unions. In 1599 a Marseille Chambre de Commerce was formed to arbitrate mercantile affairs, promote trade and lend advice on public works projects.

The first evidence of organization in Canada occurred in 1750. Some merchants of Halifax joined to form an 'Association for the Benefit of Trade'. A Committee of Trade was formed in Montreal in 1822 and Toronto organized the City of Toronto Board of Trade in 1835. Throughout the early nineteenth century, Boards of Trade and Chambers of Commerce (the names are interchangeable) were formed. They were independent groups with well defined structures and aims, working collectively to stimulate and develop their communities and create a favourable environment which would advance their own interests. Boards recognized no conflict between these objectives.

Booster Spirit

The success of one Northern city relative to another was not determined only by a convenient resource or location, but it helped in the case of Sudbury, Sault Ste. Marie, Timmins, Thunder Bay (Fort William/Port Arthur) and North Bay.

The residents of North Bay interacted with the environment, and their hopes, beliefs, energy, community spirit, initiative and adaptability influenced the rate of growth, degree of prosperity and the physical makeup of the city. An important element in the analysis of how the Board of Trade/Chamber of Commerce influenced the development of our community requires some understanding of the beliefs and activities of this organization.

Members of the Board of Trade/Chamber of Commerce believed in a concept called the "booster" spirit. From this mental mind set different ways of dealing with particular problems and opportunities emerged. Boosterism was a general theme of community growth; the idea that if a community was to become "better" it had to become "bigger." This notion was the driving force behind the Board/Chamber. There were, of course, variations in the degree of attachment to the booster spirit throughout the larger, developing communities of Northern Ontario. But 80 years later in 1974, President John Lyle was echoing similar sentiments, he said, "Chambers of Commerce are community booster organizations. We recognize that pride in one's community is an important factor in the over-all well-being and public spirit of a town or city."

North Bay, with a strategic geographical location, became a transportation centre and did not soley rely on the wealth of the hinterland's natural resources. In the early beginnings of North Bay the boosters were Anglo-Saxon Protestants who had come from southern and eastern Ontario. The possibilities of "material" success in an undeveloped region was an immediate challenge. Early promotional reports and brochures initiated by the Board of Trade measured progress in quantitative terms - numbers of rail lines, miles of streets, dollars of assessments, size of population and value of wholesale trade.

As in the other Northern Ontario towns that became cities, boards of trade were the first organizations formed to channel growth. It is interesting to note there was virturally no co-operation among other Northern Ontario cities in their dealings with railways, industry or provincial and federal governments. Each centre zealously competed with the others for economic advantage and prestige. This feeling of competiveness remains today.

But while there was a lack of cooperation among the communities of the north there was a high degree of coordination within the boards of trade. To townsmen, (dominated by men for more than 50 years), being a member of a board of trade was essential to progress and prosperity and was synonymous with good citizenship.

The boards of trade saw themselves as community builders where personal prosperity was part of public growth. There was no room for "knockers" as sceptics were known.

As for municipal government, boards of trade in Northern Ontario shared the view that business enterprise and growth of the community was interconnected. A board of trade often saw itself as the "right arm" of municipal council, using the power at various levels of government.

Such an example occurred in 1912 when a railroad strike threatened the town. The local Canadian Brotherhood of Railway Employees sent the Board of Trade a memorandum outlining their grievances concerning wages, hours and overtime pay. The CPR did not appoint a conciliation board and the railroaders went on strike. The Board of Trade said the welfare of the railway employees was very important to the community, and that the request for a board of conciliation was a reasonable request. Although highly criticized in some circles, the Board of Trade requested that the Minister of Labour appoint such a board of conciliation. The request was granted and the outcome ruled in favour of the employees.

The Board/Chamber often comprised business leaders, those involved in community politics and voluntary organizations. From the late 1890's through to the 1930's there are many examples where the mayor and councillors served (at different times) on the board of trade and vice versa. It was the businessmen who continued to gain control of the local government. So much so it was the North Bay Board of Trade that started the process to incorporate the town into a city - an event that occurred in 1925. It was a honor and an important characteristic of growth and prosperity. Respect within the rest of the province was paramount and cityhood provided a base for borrowing funds for public works (debentures) and other expenditures.

It is interesting to note that in the context of the 1930's and the Great Depression Pierre Berton describes the influence of the Dionne Quintuplets in terms of boosterism. "Apart from everything else, the quintuplets were an incredible commercial success. They had transformed the town of Callander, given a boost to North Bay and a transfusion to the Ontario tourist industry."

Spatial expansion was important to North Bay in 1968 as it amalgamated with the Townships of Widdifield and West Ferris. This was another example where the North Bay and District Chamber of Commerce supported amalgamation and began to take advantage of advertisements and promotional efforts when the new city was formed - one of the largest in Canada (area).

And boosterism has had a humorous side. One "Booster" in the 1960's was fond of remarking, "This is the best defended city in Canada." He was referring to the Bomarc missile base, the Trout Lake (SAGE) underground defence complex and the fighter squadrons of the Canadian Forces Base.

It was these types of influence that helped shape the development of North Bay. The North Bay Board of Trade/District Chamber of Commerce was not alone responsible for the growth and development of the community. It has always been interested in stimulating urban economic growth - through transportation improvements, encouraging new industries, while promoting tourism, administrative and institutional functions. But combined within a framework of geographic and economic influences it had a profound effect on many of the city's most important developments. And this is what this book is all about.

In October of 1928 the Associated Boards of Trade of Ontario held their annual convention at the Empire Hotel in North Bay. Railton photo.

Lay of the Land

When you look at the history of settlement in the North Bay area you are contemplating only a little more than one hundred years of development. The impact on the landscape of the area known as "New Ontario" remains small in comparison to the urban sprawl of the south.

The north has always conjured up visions of an untamed wilderness and the "Gateway City" has long been regarded as the jumping off spot for challenges with the landscape and the natural resources it possesses. The Board of Trade would try to capitalize on early resources to attract pioneers to the area.

In The Beginning

North Bay lies on the Canadian Shield, a rugged, hilly plateau. It is adorned with rivers and lakes as our own area attests. There are few cities anywhere built on two major waterbodies that comprise two separate drainage basins. The height of land between Lake Nipissing and Trout Lake is a recent reminder of our geologic past.

For the most part surface geology has been influenced by four periods of continental glaciation lasting for approximately 500,000 years. The last ice sheet, the Wisconsin ice mass of 10,000 years ago and the events which led to its retreat created most of our existing landforms that are visible around the city.

Geologic history indicates the front of the retreating ice mass passed from south to north during a 1,000 to 1,500-year period. Features remaining today were bulldozed by brief glacial advances and were partially or totally submerged under glacial melt waters.

Initially because of the tremendous weight of the ice, outlets were established which allowed the prehistoric shallow sea to escape via the Ottawa River. North Bay would have been the floor of a river escaping through the Mattawa Valley to the east via Parks Creek. Driving along Highway 11, south of the 11/17 interchange, rock formations indicate the islands that would have dotted the outlet. As new outlets were opened water levels dropped allowing Lake Nipissing to form its own water body.

As the glacier continued to retreat, the land was relieved of the great weight of ice pressing down upon it, a rebounding effect occurred and it started to rise. This closed off the Mattawa Valley and created a height of land between Lake Huron and the Ottawa Valley. Thereafter, Lake Nipissing drained westward. Trout Lake became part of the Ottawa River drainage basin.

Because of its geographical position the temperate climate of of our area has created a transitional forest of deciduous and coniferous trees. Its composition is no more evident than during the changing of the seasons.

Another view of the natural evolution of our earth is captured in an Ojibway legend provided by North Bayite, Wayne Bliss.

"In the beginning, the Earth was covered in water and from the sky a woman fell. Two loons that saw her falling flew under her to break her fall. Then they swam with her on their backs so as to prevent her from drowning. Eventually, they became tired of the load and a great turtle said that it would take her on his back. Finally the turtle and all the animals agreed that she should have land to live on and the turtle sent all the animals of the water to the bottom to bring up earth and then to be packed around him until it made land. Eventually the task was complete. Even today evidence of the great turtle is present, only today his great shell is known as BEDROCK."

It took a great deal of blasting to make the streets of the downtown core passable, where a rockcut is being removed, near the corner of Fraser and Main Streets. Nipissing Archives/North Bay Area Museum photo.

This bedrock is best seen as you drive through the rockcut on Thibeault Hill. It represents rock formed during the Precambrian age and is older than 570 million years. The uneven surface, characteristic of the North Bay area is typical of the glaciated Canadian Shield. When a young John Ferguson arrived in July of 1882 to lay claim to what would be the downtown area he would have discovered exposed bedrock and poorly drained, low lying areas. Arable soil would have been scarce. Early in 1883 the Canadian Pacific Railroad actually had a quarry on Main St., using the rock for their roadbed. It is one reason why the east side of Main St. is higher than the west side. Also, John Ferguson donated (for $1) the worst of his downtown lots to the various churches in the fledgling community. If you visit the sites of Trinity United, St. Andrew's and St. John's churches you will see the exposed bedrock that they sit upon. Where McIntyre bisects Fraser, Ferguson, Wlyd and Fisher Streets, blasting occured to remove rock outcroppings. In fact most of the downtown core is a small hill of bedrock. What did John Ferguson see in this townsite? The question is not answered by suitability, but due to geographic location.

Farming First

When you look at Northern Ontario most of the important settlements were developed around mining centres. One area that was successfuly settled is the irregular trough of land that connects the basin of Georgian Bay with the Ottawa River valley. This was once the outlet for the prehistoric Great Lakes that once flowed eastward into the Ottawa valley.

What the glaciers left was rounded knolls and ridges of exposed bedrock. Between these outcroppings are small plains and depressions covered with loose rock of glacial origin and mixtures of clays and silts of former lake beds. It is these areas free from boulders, with layers of clay, silt and fine sand that provided for successful agricultural settlement.

In its earliest beginnings the settlements of Rutherglen, Alderdale, Powassan, Verner, Warren, St. Charles and Noelville established stable farming communities serving logging camps with hay and oats.

Harry Yeates, who has lived all of life on the south shore of Lake Nipissing, remembers convoys of sleighs, crossing Lake Nipissing (1920's). They arrived at what is now Sunset Park onto Kennedy Avenue (now Lakeshore Drive). "Dairies and bakeries all maintained stables, and hay bales weighed 135 pounds in those days."

Agricultural beginnings are also tied to the coming of the CPR between the years 1881-1883. In 1881 there were already two decades of development with 2,300 people located near the villages of Nipissing and Mattawa. By 1891 the population of Nipissing District had increased to 12,000 most of whom lived along the new CPR line. A network of wagon and sleigh trails challenging the wilderness would become today's system of roads and pattern of settlement.

The first promotional publication issued by the Board of Trade was published in 1897 and was entitled, 'Nipissing District,' with the subtitles: With Special Reference to the Townships of Widdifield, Ferris, Bonfield, Chisholm, Phelps, Mulock, Merrick and Blyth, a description of their Soil, Climate, Products, Area, Agricultural Capabilities, Timber Resources, and general information respecting the settlement of public lands for sale, and the lands open for settlement under the "Free Grants Act."

It was just that - promotion - description of the area with pictures of prosperity. For instance, the introduction states, "The Nipissing District is capable of maintaining hundreds and thousands of people in agriculture, manufacturing and general industry." In summary, "That the district possesses all the advantages and qualities necessary to render it attractive to, and

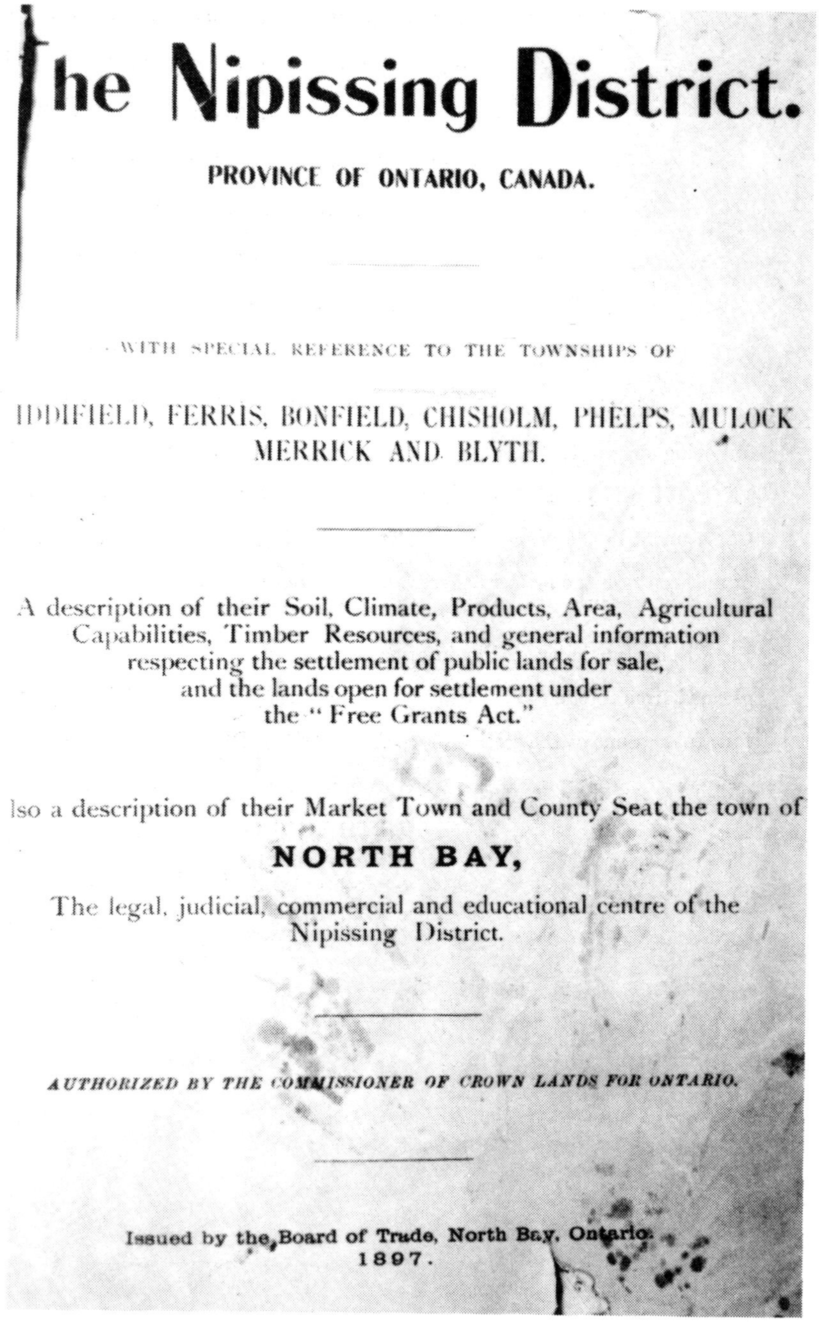

The Nipissing District.

PROVINCE OF ONTARIO, CANADA.

WITH SPECIAL REFERENCE TO THE TOWNSHIPS OF

IDDIFIELD, FERRIS, BONFIELD, CHISHOLM, PHELPS, MULOCK MERRICK AND BLYTH.

A description of their Soil, Climate, Products, Area, Agricultural Capabilities, Timber Resources, and general information respecting the settlement of public lands for sale, and the lands open for settlement under the "Free Grants Act."

lso a description of their Market Town and County Seat the town of

NORTH BAY,

The legal, judicial, commercial and educational centre of the Nipissing District.

AUTHORIZED BY THE COMMISSIONER OF CROWN LANDS FOR ONTARIO.

Issued by the Board of Trade, North Bay, Ontario.
1897.

The earliest promotional effort of the Board of Trade was published in 1897 as a guide for new businesses and pioneer families. Nipissing Archives/ North Bay Area Museum photo.

suitable for the home of the most progressive races, namely: cheapness of land, fertility of soil, first-class live stock and dairy advantages, ability to produce all the crops of the temperate zone, incalculable forest wealth, variety of industries, winter employment, good wages for labor, cheap building material, fuel for the cutting, fruit for the picking, fine fisheries, game plentiful, great range of products, good railway accomodation, water communication, religious and educational advantages, a healthy country, pure and plentiful water, regular rainfall, temperateness of climate, local market, nearness to foreign markets." It was a sentence worth reading especially if you were considering relocating to the North Bay area.

Much of the booklet compared, specifically, conditions in other areas of southern Ontario and the mid-western United States. "The winters are infinitely more pleasant and less trying than the winters in the Western States; even so far south as the states of Illinois, Missouri and Kansas; and paradise itself compared with the Dakotas and Minnesota. In the excitement that has attended the absorption of the good land in the Western States the railroad building and the rush to the cities, this northern country has been somewhat overlooked."

The booklet even answered the abundance of Cambrian Shield throughout the district. "It is not desired that anyone should settle on these ridges, on the contrary, it is desired that these rock lands should be left clothed with forests in their natural condition, for the shelter and protection of the adjacent country and the conservation of the summer rains. Taking out a few parts of the country which are not fitted for settlement, the remainder may be accurately described as well fitted for agricultural purposes."

The Ontario government, as part of their colonization program, offered free, or low-cost land to settlers along with reduced rates offered by the CPR. In many cases, the soil was found to be too thin, stony, sandy or poorly drained. Many farmsteads were abandoned and the owners would gravitate to the largest centre, North Bay, in search of employment. For many it was a time of "broken promises and shattered dreams."

One of North Bay's first dairies was located where Howard Johnson's (Empire Hotel) parking lot is located. The Central Dairy was operated by Sarah Simms and remained in operation until 1928 when it was purchased by the Davie Brothers (later Silverwoods). Ted Moseley-Williams collection.

The First Entrepreneurs

Samuel de Champlain wrote many accounts of business transactions between the French and the many different aboriginal groups he was to encounter. He first gazed across the waters of Lake Nipissing July 26th, 1615.

Champlain was typical of the early explorers in having his mind set on discovering a route to Cathay and finding gold, silver and diamonds. What he did find were natural products that could be gathered from the aboriginals. Fine furs - beaver, fox, otter and marten were in demand in Europe as the fur bearing animals were in decline in Europe in the early 1400's.

What Champlain and his contemporaries established was a trading industry with the natives that would last more than 300 years. It was a business that promoted exploration, mixed cultures, initiated the course of settlement patterns and determined the theme of politics for the French, English, Americans and our First Nations people. Jean Nicolet, the first white resident of the Nipissing area, lived with the Nipissings for nine years. The fur trading business became a reality.

As he moved up the Ottawa Valley and into the Nipissing passageway (Mattawa River, Trout Lake, La Vase portages, Lake Nipissing, French River), Champlain and his forerunner Etienne Brule met the Nipissings, the nomadic tribe that inhabited this well-travelled route. This tribe was known by other bands as the "sorcerers," well known for their trading abilities and better known for their supposed magical powers for creating lasting curses. The Nipissings ("people of the little water") had lived continuously in the Lake Nipissing area for more than 3,000 years throughout the advance and retreat of the last ice age. Most of the village sites have been found on the French River, Trout Lake and the north shore of Lake Nipissing where missionaries noted their presence in abundance.

In pre-contact years sedentary tribes such as the nearby Hurons of the Georgian Bay area did not gather enough skins for their needs. Instead they exchanged their surpluses of food with the Nipissings for furs. Archaeologists and anthropologists have proven there was an extensive Amerindian trading network in existence before the arrival of the white man. When the explorers came the natives were more than willing to deal with these new tribes that had such interesting and excellent products.

Literally, the voyageurs (licenced) and coureur de bois (unlicenced, runners of the woods) would have traded for the very furs worn by the Nipissings. History tells us the fresh beaver pelts retained coarse, outer guard hairs that were difficult to remove in the felting process.

Traders requested the used, worn furs that were softer due to the wearers' natural body oils. That is to say older clothes were worth more than new ones.

Another curious characteristic of the trading exchange was the natives' limited view of their needs. When their immediate needs were satisfied with trade goods it was difficult to motivate them to bring in more furs. This made little sense to the capitalist trader.

The Nipissings were known for their close relationship with the Hurons. The Black Robes, as they were known, the missionaries from the Society of Jesus, (Jesuits) noted the annual custom of the tribe to leave their home region and winter with the Hurons. They would take their great catches of "dore" (golden pickerel) to trade for corn.

Father Jerome Lalament, a Jesuit missionary described the Nipissings:

"The Askikwanehronons, according to our Hurons: or Nipissirinens, according to the Algonkians, form a Nation of Algonkian tongue which contains more wandering than settled people. They seem to have as many abodes as the year has seasons, in the spring a part of them remain for fishing, where they consider it best; a part go away to trade with the tribes which gather on the shore of the North or icy sea, upon which they voyage ten days, after having spent thirty days upon the rivers, in order to reach it.

"In the summer, they all gather together, on the road of the Hurons to the French, on the border of a large lake which bears their name, and is about two hundred leagues distance from Quebec, and about seventy from our Hurons; so that their principal dwelling place, is, as it were, two-thirds of the way from Quebec to the country of our Hurons.

"About the middle of autumn, they begin to approach our Hurons, upon whose lands they generally spend the winter; but before reaching them, they catch as many fish as possible, which they dry. This is the ordinary money with which they buy their main stock of corn although they come supplied with all other goods, as they are a rich people and live in comfort. They cultivate a little land near their summer dwelling; but it is more for pleasure, than for their support."

From the above we know the Nipissings inhabited the north bay of Lake Nipissing and that they were an integral link in trading with the Hurons and the Cree of James and Hudson Bays.

As middlemen they became part of a competitive trading network that involved the Dutch and English in the New York State area and the Hurons who traded with the French at Montreal, Trois Rivieres and Quebec. What evolved was a war with the Iroquois confederacy who favoured the English and Dutch trading partners. During the 1640's the Nipissings were driven from their traditional hunting and fishing grounds to the Lake Nipigon area, north of Lake Superior. Later they returned and resumed their traditional lifestyle. It is known that some Nipissings helped to defend New France from the English in 1760 during the battle at Quebec City and helped defend Canada during the war of 1812.

Heritage Appreciation

Heritage was important to the Chamber, as early as 1951 a number of members headed by Kenneth J. Barry formed the 'Nipissing Champlain Historical Society.' Their intent was to bring more attention to the famous route used by explorers and voyageurs through the series of La Vase portages and to establish a trail to promote the important era of Canadian history.

There was a resurgence of the idea in the 1960's and the historical committee of the Chamber was again very active in promoting the idea of a historical trail, from the site of Fort Laronde upstream to a re-creation of a Nipissing Indian village. Murray Leatherdale, former Chamber president, chairman of the historical committee and author of 'Nipissing from Brule to Booth' (published by the Chamber in 1975) said in correspondence to city council, "I believe that we could give a beautiful and dramatic Canadian history lesson that both our visitors and local residents would enjoy." Mr. Leatherdale believed that a newly-formed conservation authority (which the Chamber had been working towards forming) could "preserve forever a seven-mile link in the chain of water and portage, that was so important, so essential to the opening of Canada."

In 1961, a plaque commemorating the historic La Vase Portages was unveiled beside Highway #17-East and Dugas Bay on Trout Lake. The ceremony was sponsored by the Chamber and helped launch the partial brushing and signing of the historic portage over the height-of-land used by aboriginals, explorers, voyageurs and pioneers to get to Lake Nipissing.

The Chamber continued to chase the idea of recreating Fort Laronde at the mouth of the La Vase River (Premier Rd.). The former North West Company outpost was not a fort but a house and storage depot maintained by agent, Eustache de la Ronde sometime between 1811-1821. It was the first evidence of North Bay's mercantilism. It was thought the opening of a historic walking trail might coincide with the city's plan for a park at the end of Premier Road. The signing of the trail did materilize but was abandoned in the mid-1960's because vandals wrecked signs along the portage route.

Although the re-creation of the fur trading post did not come about, the Chamber supported the establishment of another historic monument (by the North Bay Historical Committee) at Champlain Park (Premier Rd) commemorating the contributions of Samuel de Champlain, Etienne Brule, the missionaries, voyageurs and the Nipissing Indians who travelled through the historic Nipissing passageway.

The steamer Booth, heeled over because of too many people on one side, on a French River excursion in 1905. Nipissing Archives/North Bay Area Museum photo.

Painting A Picture

What was North Bay like in 1894 the year the Board of Trade became a reality?

In 1894, train travellers aboard the fledgling Canadian Pacific Railway out of Montreal, and on the rival Grand Trunk Railway (GTR became the CNR) from Toronto, would emerge from a dense forest, to disembark at a frame station.

While water was added to the steam locomotive travellers would see the first evidence of what was known as "New Ontario," the government name for the vast hinterland above the borderline formed by the French River, Lake Nipissing and the Mattawa River.

Some passengers would disembark. They were probably first and second generation pioneers from Eastern Ontario or the lower Ottawa Valley, a mix of Scottish, Irish and British descent. It was probably the spring time; mosquitoes would have been annoying, however one would not have considered arriving in the winter to start a lifetime. Their belongings were sparse but their will and determination to succeed was great. They would see their first glimpses of what comprised the immense Canadian Shield. Bare rock outcroppings in the new town were visible, giving the town a hilly appearance. The wooden sidewalks on Main Street were higher on one side (east) because a CPR quarry had used the rock for the roadbed. The streets were muddy, since the location was once natural wetlands.

North Bay, incorporated in 1891, was a rough looking town, but obviously busy and intent on growing. Sawmills were billowing out clouds of steam and smoke, and the whine of the big saws could be heard throughout the original townsite that was borderd by Chippewa Creek northward to Klock Avenue (Algonquin Avenue); Worthington Street was the eastern extremity and Front St. (Oak St.) bordered the railway yards. There were good and bad places to live. By far the most ideal residential location was in the "west end", while the least desirable was on or near the poorly drained, rocky land in the "east end" near the CPR railway tracks. There was approximately two thousand people (1,726 - 1891) living in and around the village. It was a young town, the average age of men possessing property was 34.6 years, while 71.6 per cent of men were under the age of forty, with a balance of men and women in the overall population.

As a pioneer you probably headed for the Pacific Hotel (now the St. Regis) one of the only establishments that offered hardy meals and a place to stay ($2 per day). For the newcomers it was a shocking experience, the first look at a frontier town.

Looking westward they would see the sparkling waters and uninterrupted shoreline of Lake

Nipissing or possibly the rafts of timber that were towed by small steam boats. A year earlier the new arrival would have seen the John Fraser moored at the government wharf. The small steamer served lumber camps across the lake. But on November 7, 1893 a fire broke out on board and the boat sank between the Goose and Manitou Islands; twenty-one men were drowned or burned to death.

To the north a densely, forested escarpment seemed to be a barrier to the area beyond. Where would their farm be located? The visitors would wonder how farms could produce anything worth growing.

Community Concerns

North Bay has attained a few milestones as a municipality. In 1882 it was incorporated as a village, part of Widdifield Township. In 1891 North Bay received town status and in 1925 was designated a city. In 1968, amalgamation brought together the Townships of Widdifield and West Ferris with the city.

The evolution of North Bay from a village to a town was linked to the development of the Board of Trade in 1894. North Bay was becoming a regional service centre because of the rise of mercantilism. Railroads from the south and east had merged to make the village an important rail centre. Establishing itself as a town, the third in Northern Ontario (Port Arthur, 1884, Sault Ste. Marie, 1887), was a monumental achievement and was considered a prestigious standing within New Ontario. When you were a town you were something.

The early bylaws established by town council indicate the concerns of early merchants. They wanted the new council to spend their money wisely.

"All members of council having made declaration of office the council was thus organized...," are the first words entered by clerk J.G. Cormack in the minutes of the inaugural meeting of the Town of North Bay, 11:00 a.m., January 19, 1891.

At this time, council was faced with controlling 500 acres of unserviced land with a tax assessment of $302,461, it was forced to borrow $500 from the Bank of Ottawa in Pembroke to cover expenditures. One of the reasons the town was established was to stem complaints received from the larger geographical area of Widdifield Township (of which the village of North Bay was a part prior to 1891). Taxpayers were upset with the majority of tax revenue being spent on North Bay. To help North Bay survive and provide a financial base for eventual public utilities (steam generated electricity was privately owned by the new mayor, John Bourke) tax rates were levied to its residents. On each dollar of property there was a

One of the earliest photos of downtown North Bay taken during the Orange Parade of 1894. It's an important photo because it indicates the low, muddy areas of Main St. The tower in the center of the photo was part of Our Lady of the Lakes Church (now Lefebvre's). North Bay Area Museum photo.

general levy of one and a half cents, both school boards levied the same rate.

Concerns were raised about the downtown area. One petition asked for a twelve-foot plank sidewalk along the new post office (corner of Fraser/Main). Poor drainage was a problem with frequent references to muddy streets.

To help consumers Bylaw Number Ten obligated each shopkeeper to retain measuring scales on their premises. Petty trades selling wares door-to-door were disallowed by Bylaw Number Twelve, and these service and sales people were identified as "non-permanent residents." Convicted offenders could be sent to the "common goal with or without hard labour for a period not exceeding six months."

Although there were no motorized vehicles Bylaw Number Nine states: "No person shall place any carriage, cart, wagon, sled or sleigh on any street unless hitched to a horse." The horse also needed a licence costing 24 cents.

There weren't many cars on the Main Street in 1910 - 1920. The large white building on the left was the Post Office at the corner of Fraser and Main Streets. Nipissing Archives/North Bay Area Museum photo.

Bylaw Number Five addressed the moral behavior of townsfolk. It states: "No person shall be drunk or be guilty of drunkeness, profane swearing, obscene, blasphemous, or grossly insulting language." In a subsection of the bylaw there is reference to the "keeping of a common bawdy house for the purpose of fornicating, lewdness, indecency and gambling." Bylaw Number Six identifies a $100 licence needed for the sale of "intoxicating liquors in taverns and shops (grocery stores)."

Such were the early concerns of the citizens and town council. Three years would pass before businessmen and professionals would join to form a more formidable and organized voice. North Bay required many improvements, including waterworks, power facilities, a sewage system, street clearance and drainage, fire protection, new housing and regulations to check growth. In dealing with these situations town council was aided by the Board of Trade which would consider itself the "true custodians of civic property and order."

"With the above gentlemen as the moving spirits, the future prosperity of the town is a foregone conclusion."

The above quote appeared in the North Bay Times newspaper following the election of officers of the Board of Trade, October 19, 1894. The "gentlemen" who were the subject of the comment made the first board of directors. They were David Purvis, president, (owner of large hardware business); J.G Cormack, vice-president (druggist, town clerk); D.J. McKeown, secretary, (CPR agent); W. Martin, treasurer; and directors, A.G. Browning (North Bay's first lawyer), Richard Bunyon, (flour and feed store), John Bourke, (developer), L.P. Synder (banker), William Doran, (Stipendiary Magistrate), Michael Brennan, (dry goods and tailoring), J.M. McNamara, T. Darling, T.N. Coglan, (CPR bridge and building master), J. Deegan (boots and shoe repair), Dr. A. McMurchy (CPR physician), and Dr. J.B. Carruthers (North Bay's second doctor).

Board of Trade members included: John Ferguson, A.F. Doyle, Andrew McIntosh, J. Dunlop, W.J. Parsons, B.M. Mulligan, J.T. Lovell, Adam Torrence, William McKenzie, James Halpenny, John Blanchette, D. McIntyre, Robert Rankin, W.A. Martyn, John Allard, Geroge Pay, J. W. McDonald, A. McLellan, E.W. Ross, G.F. Turner, and D.H. Barr.

They were the leading business and professional men of North Bay, most of them came soon after the CPR was built and were the founding families of the city. As you drive along the streets of North Bay their names remain prominent reminders of its past.

In 1887 William McKenzie had one of the first general stores on Oak Street. He would become mayor and act as the town's customs official. North Bay Area Museum photo.

One of the original "boosters" of the community was the Richardson family pictured in 1897. Nipissing Archives/North Bay Area Museum photo.

A typical small home on McIntyre Street East in the 1920's. This shows a Salvation Army Captain and his family on the site of the present day Salvation Army building. Nipissing Archives/North Bay Area Museum photo.

The choir is an important part of any church, this photo shows the 1898 Methodist choir (now Trinity United Church). Nipissing Archives/North Bay Area Museum photo.

A North Bay lacrosse team in 1915 when the sport was very popular. Nipissing Archives/North Bay Area Museum photo.

Two girls on a Sunday outing in 1910. Nipissing Archives/North Bay Area Museum photo.

The Capitol Theatre was an arts centre. In 1931 the community put on the musical - Mikado. Nona and Bill Schorse collection.

Key To Continuing Education

The North Bay Public Library has had a colorful history and its earliest beginnings coincide with the early mandate of the Board of Trade - serving the community.

The history of North Bay is undoubtedly a result of the Canadian Pacific Railway. Making the village a division point on the main line brought services that resulted in bringing company officials to the community.

One man, D.J. McKeown is well known to early North Bay as he came to the pioneer settlement in 1883 as the CPR agent in charge of timber shipments. He became the secretary of the Board of Trade in 1894. One of his first interests in working for the betterment of the community and CPR families was the initiation of a railway library in 1890. The collection of books valued at $500 in the 1890's was housed in a building that was part of the "red row," on Oak St. It is known there was a reading room for employees and family members. It was heavily used by transitory workers whose homes were not in North Bay. This service was one that early residents wanted for their use.

A subscription library was developed charging members one dollar per year. Money taken in was used for the enrichment of all as community concerts were staged.

Along with L.P. Synder, first manager of the Traders Banks and A.G. Browning, Crown Attorney and Mr. McKeown, formed a Board committee to start a library for the townsfolk. Mr. Browning would serve as President of the Board of Trade in 1906-08. Mr. McKeown decided the CPR book collection should be part of the new library that was located in the Cormack Block on Main St. East. It opened October 12, 1895 with a membership of 270 and book stock of 577, it remained open two evenings a week and on Saturday. In those days, librarian Miss A. Begg was the only person allowed to take books from the shelves. Members were kept abreast of the collection through a printed catalogue of books and periodic supplements.

An indication of the library's popularity is evident in the $296.70 worth of fees collected. Many Board of Trade members were avid readers, including: Judge J.A. Valin, Dr. Archibald McMurchy, first physician (CPR employed) in the community; J.W. Richardson, tinsmith and hardware owner, E.W. Ross, jewellery store owner and Robert Rankin, wholesaler and councillor.

Town council was delighted with the progress of the library. With a resolution by the Board of Trade a substantial sum of $250 was given to the library in 1896. Another $255 was chipped in by the provincial government. The reading room was a regular meeting room for the Board of Trade.

A friend of many libraries, financier Andrew Carnegie made his presence known to town council with an offer to provide money for the building and furnishing of a library. The conditions were that council provide a suitable site and provide an annual grant. In 1913 the sum of $16,357 was received from the Carnegie Fund to fund the first such library in Northern Ontario. By 1914 a new library opened at the corner of McIntyre and Wyld Streets and remained until it was demolished after a half-century of service.

The Carnegie Public Library, a first for Northern Ontario, was built in 1912 where the City Hall is located. Nipissing Archives/North Bay Area Museum photo.

In 1956 the provincial director of library services advised the community the library was too small for the size of the city and recommended land be acquired for the building of a new facility. The present library opened in 1966 on Worthington St. East., next to what would become the new city hall, which opened in 1978.

Helping to make the fledgling community a little less "rough" was the North Bay High School's Literary Society in 1910. Nipissing Archives/North Bay Area Museum photo.

Promoting A Privilege

The year 1989 marked the 100th anniversary of the operation of the Nipissing District Court House. By the winter of 1990 it had met its demise, a landmark turned into rubble.

Although its construction occurred before the formation of the Board of Trade, the designation of North Bay as the County Town in 1895 was not a foregone conclusion. History indicates the coercive efforts of the Board of Trade swayed election votes in North Bay's favour.

In 'A Judicial Story', an article authored by George E. Wallace, Q.C., he explains the behind-the-scenes actions that helped cement North Bay as the admiministrative centre of Nipissing District.

In 1889 an Act was passed creating Nipissing, a district for purposes of provincial parliamentary representation in Toronto. The Act removed the district from the Riding of Mr. Thomas Murray, Member of Provincial Parliament for Renfrew. However, perhaps to console Mr. Murray in his loss of this important territory, it was in the same year that the Crown purchased from him the site of the court house. Mr. Murray had purchased the land during the early 1880's when the CPR was considering North Bay as a railway divisional point. Full credit must be given to Mr. Murray's political powers of persuasion when one realizes the property was purchased and that the court house building was erected while North Bay was still part of the judicial district of Parry Sound!

As the formidable businessmen and professionals of North Bay started to flex their political will through the recently formed Board of Trade they realized the importance of securing such a position as County Town.

In 1895, during the reign of Sir Charles Tupper, the federal District of Nipissing was created. This immense tract of land extended from just south of Mattawa to Hudson Bay and from Chapleau to the Quebec border. Mattawa was the largest community in the District. Both the Provincial Member of Parliament, John Loughlin and Federal member, J.B. Klock, first representatives of both legislatures came from nearby Mattawa.

Sturgeon Falls had also progressed as a lumbering community, being second in size to Mattawa, North Bay was third and Sudbury was the smallest. When the question of the location of a County Town came up for decision, the three largest centres felt that they were entitled. North Bay based its claim largely on the existing court house.

The struggle became a real battle between the three communities. And as Mr. Wallace states:

"...which proves history is educational. Finally the government decided to save itself from further embarrassment and to call for a vote."

On March 14, 1895 this matter was submitted to the electorate. On the first ballot North Bay won by 108 votes under circumstances considered suspicious to the other municipalities. Mattawa called for a recount and then another vote which was held on July 11, 1895. At this point Sturgeon Falls dropped out, throwing its support to Mattawa, all but 24 votes that is. As fate would have it these 24 votes cast at Sturgeon Falls in favour of North Bay created a majority of eight for North Bay. And as Mr. Wallace said, "North Bay has just been waiting to show its gratitude to Sturgeon Falls ever since."

Where did all those extra votes come from anyway? Perhaps Board of Trade President, David Purvis (Conservative), was atoning for his recent defeat of 1890 at the hands of John Loughrin (Liberal) in the provincial runoff. Also, North Bay council minutes show that a grant of $1,000 was made towards defraying the expenses in connection with a "County Town" election, and if necessary a further grant was to be authorized.

A review of the balloting in the second contest showed that Mattawa had cast fewer votes on the second occasion when it was making an all-out effort to win, than on the first.

In Anson Gard's, 1909, book, 'Gateway to Silverland' he said, "I asked a good citizen, why this difference?" and he said: 'I guess a lot of the first voters couldn't stand a resurrection.' I have often wondered what he meant - rather I did wonder, till another good citizen got to enumerating the various residences of the voters: 'There was,' he said, 'the first ward, the second ward, the third ward (North Bay was originally formed on the Murray, Metcalfe and Ferguson ward system) and the cemetery."

Under a subtitle entitled, 'A Long, Wild Race for a Vote,' Gard says, "Some of the incidents of the day (second voting day) are really good enough." Possibly the most dramatic was of a train crew of five that raced back to North Bay to vote (they had picked up a passenger who was persuaded to vote).

As told to Anson Gard, one of the trainmen said, "We could hardly hope to make it, but there wasn't one of us but was willing to go the limit trying. We bit off the miles like eatin' pie...and as we swung into town, boxes blazing 'n coal nearly all gone, we turned the train over to the boys waiting and in carriages were driven on the dead run for the polls fifteen minutes to the good."

How important was this political victory. In the Board of Trade's first "boosting" publication, 'Nipissing District,' 1897, it stated: "Being the district town, corresponding to a county town where there is county organization, it is, in addition to being the commercial and educational centre of the district, also the legal centre." People went to great lengths to exercise their political franchise.

It was horse and pumper in the early 1900's for North Bay's Fire Department. Nipissing Archives/North Bay Area Museum photo.

North Bay's "finest" are seen outside Ferguson Hardware on Main Street near the turn of the century. Nipissing Archives/North Bay Area Museum photo.

Cottage Hospital

When North Bay became an incorporated town in 1891 there was no hospital in the young community.

There were few doctors, the first two professionals, Drs. McMurchy and Carruthers had arrived with the CPR and were on the first directorship of the Board of Trade in 1894.

In the early minutes of town council the Board of Trade requested council to act on building a medical facility. This was no easy undertaking given the lack of tax revenue and the immediacy of the project.

The history of North Bay's first hospital is very definitely bound up with the "Victorian Order of Nurses for Canada," under whose auspices it came into being. The entire history can be found in the booklet, 'Eighty Years of Progress - North Bay Civic Hospital, 1904-1984,' by Sydna Shorse.

North Bay, as a frontier community was a perfect candidate for the "cottage hospital" designed by Lady Aberdeen, wife of Canada's Governor-General from 1894 to 1898. As she visited rural parts of Canada, Lady Aberdeen felt the "Institute of Queen's Nurses," founded in 1887 as a tribute to Queen Victoria, would provide the needed medical help. The order was founded on the rules subscribed to by Miss Florence Nightingale. Many changes were required to adapt the scheme to Canada's pioneer hinterland.

A plan was evolved to create an Order of Visiting Nurses (V.O.N.) and also to use small homes or erect inexpensive cottage hospitals. With just a few beds this facility and two or three nurses could receive patients. Local citizens including members from the Board of Trade (W. McKenzie, W.A.Smith, T.N. Coglan, Dr. Carruthers, Dr. McMurchy) formed a district cottage hospital committee. They went to Ottawa to meet with Charlotte Macleod, Chief Superintendent of the V.O.N., who had studied under Florence Nightingale in England. North Bay followed the example and was one of the first communities in the province to establish a V.O.N. hospital.

In 1900 the V.O.N., through Charlotte Macleod applied to North Bay council for a grant. Council agreed to a grant of $100 to be paid in quarterly instalments. This was found to be insufficient and in the following year a request for $150 was applied for. The application was denied and the grant was maintained at the former level. Clearly tax levies were scarce in the young community.

A letter from Lady Minto was received at town council in 1901 outlining a grant the town could have for the development of a hospital. It stated the V.O.N. would be willing to build a hospital at a cost of $3,000 providing the town would provide a site and maintain the hospital. Records indicate council waited until Miss Macleod was contacted and came to North Bay for a presentation, July 11, 1902. Apparently she was persuasive as council struck a special meeting. It was decided that an annual grant of $300 was to be spent for maintenance "provided said amount is required to defray running expenses."

What possessed council to choose the site at the top of Klock Avenue (Algonquin Ave.)? It was not easy to reach. The road grade of today is no indication of yesteryear. Council spent $500 to buy the small piece of land from John Murray, brother and partner of Thomas Murray, MP for the riding of Nipissing.

The steep hill was the bane of many of the first drivers of motorized vehicles in North Bay. Many stalled on the way up and it was a well known fact that the granting of a driver's licence depended on one's ability to manipulate the hill. Walking up and down the hill was difficult particularly in winter, and a board sidewalk was considered treacherous on any winter's day. At the same time it had a beautiful view of Lake Nipissing.

The temporary hospital - The Queen Victoria Hospital of North Bay - was in operation in 1903 with Miss Kellman and one other nurse in attendance. Before the end of the year, a total of 130 patients had been cared for. Margaret Kellman, one of the nurses, was identified in the list of "original" V.O.N. nurses for all of Canada.

The following year saw the commencement of a Training School for Nurses. Also, a series of typhoid outbreaks struck northeastern Ontario and helped launch the hospital's busy career as a medical facility. It was a difficult time as 116 typhoid patients from the mining camps of Cobalt made their way to North Bay.

A series of additions occurred until 1920. Funding of new wards was through sponsorship. Wards were furnished and maintained by A.G. Browning, G.W. Lee (chairman of the T&NO), John Ferguson, Masonic Order, Eastern Star, I.O.D.E. and St. Andrew's Presbyterian (later St. Andrew's United Church). By 1931 Queen Victoria Memorial Hospital had become the reponsibility of the North Bay Hospital Commission and was renamed the Civic General Hospital. In the same year on October 7, the Most Reverend D.J. Scollard, D.D. officially opened a ninety-bed hospital on the present site of St. Joseph's Hospital.

In 1949 the city asked the Government of Ontario permission to build a modern, 100 bed civic hospital which would open April 8, 1951.

The former hospital on Algonquin had been turned into a hotel and became a favourite dining spot and location for wedding receptions, (refurbished by Mike Zaversnuke), until it closed in 1961. It was torn down in 1969 and became a parking lot. Our hospitals serve us well. And only the people who have worked diligently to create a new facility know how hard it is to bring a concept to reality.

Once a year the Odd Fellows led by a bank would march to the Union Cemetery to hold a memorial service - Decoration Sunday - for departed members. The sister organization - the Rebekahs were taken by cars (1930 photo). The Queen Victoria Hospital is on the right. Joan Holmes - Nipissing Rebekah Lodge collection.

An important early North Bay photo because it shows the CNR trestle under construction with "priest's hill" (Knock Avenue, now Algonquin Avenue) in the background. Nipissing Archives/North Bay Area Museum.

Founding Father

The 1925 Old Home Week program - the celebration when North Bay became a city - describes our founding father: "He's a hustler, an animated steam engine in trousers. When you want action page John Ferguson."

As one of the community's first pioneers he rose to help form the Board of Trade as one of the driving forces in turning wilderness into cityhood. As a nineteen year old he is remembered as someone who acted on "inside information" and "was in the right place at the right time."

Which Way To Go?

To look at the first pages of North Bay's history we must look at the beginnings of the CPR. Even as the formation of the CPR was passed by parliament on February 15, 1881, a route west was being built up the Ottawa valley. The Canada Central Railway (CCR) owned by Duncan McIntyre was on its way towards Mattawa; it was being financed by government subsidies. Duncan McIntyre would soon become part of the CPR syndicate of George Stephen, Donald Smith and others.

The CPR was still unsure of where the exact route should proceed westwards, it designated its eastern terminus near the north-east shore of Lake Nipissing. In fact, engineer and surveyor, Sir Sandford Fleming had insisted: "Choose what route you please, but you must reach the north shore of Nipissing." These prophetic words are inseparably linked with the origin and destiny of North Bay.

As work progressed during the years of 1878-1881, Mr. McIntyre bestowed the name of Callander, his and his nephew John Ferguson's, birthplace in Scotland, upon the indeterminable location where construction would stop. There was no rush to get there because the location offered no financial incentive for development. By June of 1881 and upon selling the CCR to the CPR, Duncan McIntyre became a vice-president of the CPR syndicate.

The CCR had originally surveyed the railroad to travel south of Lake Nipissing towards Georgian Bay, crossing the lower French River. At the same time the Grand Trunk Railroad (GTR) out of Toronto was also interested in joining the CPR at the hypothetical location of Callander. The GTR was the second largest and ambitious railway scheme in Canada, it considered the CPR to be an important feeder line for its own agenda of economic interests.

The Montreal-based CPR was in no hurry to join with the GTR. So much so that it took a few years before the GTR would be allowed to join the CPR in North Bay. Nipissing Junction was developed for this purpose as the GTR's terminus.

Nipissing Village, another potential division point for the CPR, was already in existence by 1880 with a few hundred people and a town survey expecting 15,000 residents. In addition, the CPR received their right-of-way for free and establishing any division point would require buying or expropriating acres of costly land. With Sandford Fleming's wish they proceeded towards Lake Nipissing avoiding an extensive detour and the GTR. The mythical Callander would change locations twice (Callander was located at what would become Rutherglen and Bonfield) before becoming the village's name already started on the south-east bay of Lake Nipissing (now Callander). Most importantly, the operating distance of 100 miles for required fuel and water would be the next major stop to be designated. Leaving Chalk River, the last developed refuelling stop, the next 100-mile interval bypassed Mattawa and Nipissing. It was somewhere on what was known as the "great north bay" of Lake Nipissing.

Family Ties

James Worthington's men, working on the Canada Central Extension - as it was called - reached the Rutherglen area in the spring of 1881. The first spike of the CPR was unceremoniously hammered into place marking an end with a beginning.

A far visioned, young man of nineteen had been dispatched from Mattawa on a two-day journey to reach the railroad crew pushing the railroad right-of-way along a roughly surveyed route.

John Thompson, CPR general storekeeper at Mattawa had a hand in shaping the destiny of John Ferguson. It was in answer to his call for a volunteer to take the mail into the bush that the latter headed north. "Johnny", as he was called, had left the family farm in Bromley Township, County of Renfrew, with a team of horses looking for work. His mother's brother, Duncan McIntyre, under contract (CCR) to Sir John A. Macdonald's government had warned all of his relatives that they must not seek employment on the job, else he would have added to his many worries the charge of nepotism.

A kind friend, smuggled his name on the payroll of the D.McIntyre Co., without his uncle's knowledge. John Ferguson spent several months delivering mail along the railroad line from Bissett's Creek, through Deux Rivieres and on to Mattawa and Callander. He was handy with his horses and was the first mail carrier to lead his team the whole route through the wilderness. Always ahead of schedule he would journey two-three days ahead of the work gang to the engineers that were roughing-out the right-of-way. Maybe it was this abundance of time or maybe it was inside information that set the scene for what was to come.

In a interview with John Ferguson many years later, (Canadian Courier, newspaper, May 13, 1911) it was revealed what had transpired. It was a tidy bit of work he did with his axe, after jumping his job and selecting the site for North Bay. When William Van Horne arrived on his inspection of the roadbed he found young Ferguson "squatting" on 288 acres (mining claim) of which the CPR wanted forty acres for station and yards. Ferguson later admitted he hadn't the $288 handy and mortgaged his horses to raise the wherewithal to buy the 288 acres.

The CPR had had some annoying experiences with individuals and municipalities over the right of way and Van Horne asked John Ferguson to go to Montreal so that they could raise terms. Poor Fergsuon might as well have been asked to visit the moon in his financial state of collapse, a passage to Montreal was beyond his means. No sooner was this difficulty solved than the question of clothes arose, which, too, was quickly settled by an order on the company's stores.

"Arrayed in clothes that shrieked with their newness, Ferguson stepped off the train at Montreal, completing the longest railway trip of his life. He wondered a little when told to be at the company's office at 12 o'clock - an hour at which he knew that people should eat instead of discussing questions of the moment. Undaunted by city people's strangeness he was there on time and found there men who are immortalized in Canadian railway history."

"Young man," said Van Horne, "we have been held up so much by individuals and others that we have decided to put your case in the hands of a board of arbitration, and we name R.W. Scott as our arbitrator, and ask you to name yours, the two to name a third."

"Sir," replied Ferguson, "I don't think your arbitrator would rob a yeoman of his right and I nominate the same man."

After smelling salts had been applied, Mr. R.B. Angus said: "In our troubled experience you are the first man to suggest that we (CPR) might be honest."

Mr. Scott visited North Bay and awarded Mr. Ferguson $2,500 - a fortune for him and the times. It is known the CPR made a stipulation that the note was not to be cashed for one year. And although he had to wait the investment would eventually make him a millionaire, mostly made in the development of the community. He later became known as the "pioneer real estate dealer."

Mr. Ferguson served 18 years on council, and as mayor for four consecutive years, 1919-1922 (one year terms). He was President of the Board of Trade for several years, and was chairman of the outstanding Old Home Week of 1925. He lived with his wife Jenny and family in a house set well back from McIntyre St. West, on the present site of the Ascot Motor Inn.

It has never been determined what information Duncan McIntyre gave his nephew, but we do know that one of our main streets bears the uncle's name. Thirty-one years after the death of John Ferguson official recogniton of Mr. Ferguson's accomplishments was made in 1977. A monument was placed at his grave site in Union Cemetery.

It was a sorry day in 1938 when the Queen's Hotel (one of the earliest hotels) burned across from the Post Office (Fraser and Main Streets). Nipissing Archives/North Bay and Area Museum photo.

One of North Bay's early landmarks, the Canadian Pacific transportation building, near Main and Fraser Streets, burned down in 1962. Nipissing Archives/North Bay Area Museum.

The long building at the left was a livery stable at the corner of Cassells and Main Streets circa 1910. Nipissing Archives/North Bay Area Museum photo.

Indian Village.

Coast to Coast, C.N.R.

Old Home Week Parade.

It was a week to remember as North Bay became a city in 1925. These photos indicate the community spirit of the day. Nipissing Archives/North Bay Area Museum photos.

Early Marketing

North Bay has always been progressive. With a diversified economy, growth has occurred without the boom and bust cycle of being tied to resource extraction.

A few years ago the city's administration requested submissions for a new logo and slogan to be implemented for future public relations and marketing strategies. For most of our past, North Bay has been known as the "Gateway of the North," capitalizing on its past prominence as a transportation and service centre. The Board/Chamber has always used the words to promote business and tourism. After receiving submissions and considering public sentiment towards retaining our community slogan, the city introduced a slight change, "Gateway to Opportunity."

Early promotional efforts (1905 and 1913/14) included literature authored by the Board of Trade that served as a prospectus for potential businesses wanting to locate in the "frontier" town.

The booklets, compiled by A.C.(Cecil) Rorabeck (pharmacist, known as druggist) are some of the earliest glimpses of what North Bay looked like to thousands of pioneers headed west and north. Both booklets were simply entitled 'North Bay,' with the 1913/14 subtitle: 'Illustating Commercial, Religious, Educational, Residential Features of North Bay - Gateway of the Rich and Fertile Northland.' The word "prospect" appears in both introductions and remains the key word in inviting readers to discover what North Bay and New Ontario was all about.

In placing these booklets next to the most recent promotional literature it is certainly obvious that snappy graphics and pictorial layouts help in projecting the desired image. Despite the time lapse, the same approach was used by Mr. Rorabeck - pictures of the lifestyle of a community bent on being progressive. Black and white photographs (many of which show the earliest glimpses of North Bay) show people fishing on the French River, picnicking on Trout Lake, shots of our churches and neighbourhoods and commercial buildings - many of which have left our cityscape. For instance, a large facility, the New Ontario Brewing Co., (now Rahnmet location on the waterfront) dominated the lakeshore until it was destroyed by fire in 1915.

What prompted Mr. Rorabeck to take on such a task for the Board of Trade is not apparent. Certainly it was self-serving as pictures of his home and the interior of his businesses appear in the booklets. But it was the Board's intent - as other board of trade - to "boost" the

North Bay had its own brewery. The New Ontario Brewing Co. was located where Rahnmet is now on the waterfront.
Nipissing Archives/North Bay Area Museum photo.

community's services and facilities. This was particularly important in New Ontario for attracting businesses and new residents. Many references are made to the "new" schools, hospital and commercial buildings.

We do know Mr.Rorabeck was a forward thinking individual. His store - The Nipissing Drug Store (later to become Harris Drug Store in 1932) - was one of the most prominent businesses on Main St. He was also a cyclist, one of the best in the north, practising on a cinder track on Regina St. He also encouraged the fledgling Bell Telephone Company to locate services within his store in 1902. As their agent, Mr. Rorabeck created a 30 subscriber, 50-line switchboard. Mr. Rorabeck also had his own patented medicine for colds. It was labelled "110" and the name originated from the proprietor's own phone number and a CPR switching engine. As one of early North Bay's leading businesses he became part of an executive committee that made North Bay a city in 1925.

Great Works

Both booklets can be considered as rare, local resources. They are the only organized record of how North Bay appeared and what developments occured. In the opening texts of both, they laud the benefits of being situated on the "great transcontinental ocean to ocean Canadian Pacific Railway," and the terminal points for the Grand Trunk, Temiskaming and Northern Ontario Railways.

Both booklets predict the commencement of the construction of the Georgian Bay Ship Canal - a mammoth undertaking to link the Ottawa River and Georgian Bay. It was stated, "When these great works are completed, North Bay will be a shipping point second to no inland point in the Dominion."

Regarding homes and businesses the booklets promote the brick construction of buildings, this being a sign of economic prosperity when compared with many developing communities with only wood-frame construction. "The homes of our citizens (many still remain on McIntyre St.) are the wealth, faith and architectural taste of the owners."

Other important and progressive undertakings by the town council are described such as the "septic tank sewerage" and the "changing of the source of water supply from Lake Nipissing to Trout Lake, constructing a large reservoir on a mountain to hold millions of gallons of water; this at an elevation higher than the highest building in town, will give a water works system superior to anything we know of."

In the 1913-14 booklet under the heading of 'To Manufacturers and Capitalists,' the invitation to locate to North Bay is made. "North Bay affords the biggest opportunity for the profitable investment of capital in Canada today. Cheap electric power, abundant raw material at hand, exceptional shipping facilities, large home market and new and virgin field for manufacturers, opening up and ever-widening in the new districts being opened up by the construction of the National Transcontinental Railway and Canadian Northern Railway. New towns are growing up and the agricultural lands of the Great Clay Belt are being developed by a good class of settlers. North Bay is the key to the vast treasurehouse of Northern Ontario with its wealth of natural resources."

Recent promotional efforts by the city have included the message, "begin to discover," summarizing some of the ambitious projects that are reshaping the cityscape. In the early 1900's this was only a little different from the future wish, "Come see us, and if possible remain with us, become one with us, and help us." These thoughts still hold true.

Harvey Burrows' grocery store on Cassells Street circa 1918. Nipissing Archives/North Bay Area Museum photo.

Grand Canal

Ships the length of two football fields crossing Lake Nipissing laden with grain from the prairies. This vision at one time almost became a reality for the Board of Trade.

The proposed Georgian Bay Ship Canal was promoted as a project compared to the magnitude of the Panama Canal. In the original concept the waterway would have allowed Great Lakes' freighters to travel directly from Lake Huron to Montreal. Later it was changed to access the east end of Lake Nipissing (Deep Water Point) where five railway lines would access the port and travel to Toronto and Montreal.

It is a project that has been bantered about for more than one hundred years. For the Board of Trade it became a flagship idea that remained a major focus of its efforts for the first three decades of the century. Today, the remnants of the grandiose idea remain a popular scheme in the minds of those who believe access for pleasure boaters should be provided via the French River to Georgian Bay.

As early as 1837, the Family Compact members of the Assembly of Upper Canada ordered a survey of the possible route. The War of 1812 was still fresh in the minds of the politicians and an inland waterway would skirt American influence.

Canada's first Prime Minister, Sir John A. Macdonald, recognized the potential of the project: "The Ottawa Ship Canal and the Pacific Railroad must be constructed and no voice should be raised against the great national work which would open the western states and the colonies to the seaboard."

There was a number of advantages claimed for the proposed ship canal. It was the shortest route from the upper Great Lakes to the ocean harbour of Montreal. The northern route, being sheltered and cooler than the lower Great Lakes, would enable grain and cattle to be shipped in better condition. For shippers of the day it would translate into lower insurance rates on commodities.

Field Work

The surveyed waterway was essentially a scheme to canalize a number of rivers and lakes which exist along the former voyageur fur trading route (Nipissing Passageway - French River, Lake Nipissing, Mattawa River).

In 1904 the Department of Public Works was instructed to undertake a detailed field study of the route. The finished report of 1907 included a geological survey of rock formations, depth soundings of Lake Nipissing and engineering details of proposed dams and canals. The original 600-page document contains a wealth of detail and gives evidence of impressive study. The navigable waterway was estimated to be 70 kilometers long.

One of the biggest engineering stumbling blocks was the area between Lake Nipissing and Trout Lake. It was necessary to overcome the height of land between the two lakes (two drainage systems), through the creation of a lift lock, 202 metres long, 20 metres wide. If this lock had been constructed it would be located just south of the West Ferris Arena on Gertrude St. In conjunction with this, was a canal that was to be more than 100 meters wide and two kilometers long, that would run from Jennings Lake (Highway 11-South) to a location west of First Rocky Point (Parsons Ave.) The engineers saw the need for a railway terminal (approximately located at Tweedsmuir Public School) and a coal-fired generating plant to be located on the south side of the lock (North Bay Mall).

From the report, the engineers stated that a total of eight single and three double locks were needed in the Nipissing District to connect the various bodies of water. There would have been 11 changes of water levels ranging from three to 19 meters. In conclusion the study stated, "...the probable cost of a deep waterway can be established for $100 million, the work taking 10 years to complete."

Economic Benefit

Although the Georgian Bay Ship Canal was one way to foster nationalism it was a matter of economics that initiated the North Bay Board of Trade to lobby for the project.

With the movement of cattle, grain, lumber and minerals through the Nipissing Passageway, a significant impact would have been created in the area. North Bay would have become the logical location for a variety of processing plants. Goods manufactured in the area would have been transported to lucrative Southern Ontario markets.

One of Canada's earliest lobby movements, The Northern Associated Boards of Trade and The Associated Boards of Trade of Ontario (57 members) journeyed to Ottawa as an Ontario delegation in January of 1919 to present a document: 'The French River Improvement and Power Scheme - A Booklet Devoted to Economic Transportation.'

In essence it was politically and physically motivated by the North Bay Board of Trade. Much of the organization of the booklet was attributed to North Bayites, Dr. J.B. MacDougall, H.M. Anderson, R.A. Tyner and Cyril T. Young.

In the 59-page booklet there is a persuasive presentation on the merits of developing the French River, it is the equivalent of today's "needs" study. It is important to note that the original scheme of linking the Ottawa River had been dropped in favour of linking Georgian Bay to Lake Nipissing with North Bay as a port.

In the joint chambers' booklet they are adamant about the amount of employment it will create. "It is the only work that will afford immediate employment to 10,000 men now being discharged at the Nobel Explosives (north of Parry Sound), Sudbury nickel plants and several other war industries, and to the 4,000 Northern Ontario men returning daily from France and Flanders, and failing to find work to support their families."

Environmental concerns were not in the forefront of anyone's minds. "The three locks overcome 69 ft. 5 in. fall and generate 35,394 h.p. urgently needed in the North Bay-Sudbury district. Reports show that sales of power to mines, smelters and industries will pay five per cent interest on cost of construction."

"Standing white and red pine mainly owned by the Crown, will be enhanced in value of $5,000,000 and spruce to be made into paper at New Ontario's large paper mills will be enhanced in value of $25,000,000 due to water-borne rates."

"Mill imports which are mainly coal, will have savings due to water-borne rates of $10,000,000 in twenty-five years, which is assumed as the life of the mill, although it will be longer. It is extremely improbable that any section of Canada or the United States is as rich in natural resources as the section demanding water-borne traffic for its exports and imports, for it is rich in all latent resources of field, or mine and of forest."

In the booklet's Summary of Merits of French River Improvement, the scope of the project is stated, "Construction is extremely simple. There are no engineering difficulties. It can be completed in two years." But it was not to be. Practical and political considerations got in the way.

The mega project's demise can be attributed to the might of the powerful railway conglomerates of the day; they had their own visions of transportation. The technology to construct the plan was in place, the Suez and Panama Canals were already completed. Railways believed it was better to lay down railway tracks, rather than try to blast through the Canadian Shield. Smaller canal schemes that had previously been constructed throughout North America were not turning profits. In 1994 terms, the cost of building the waterway would have approached $3-billion. All were good reasons for not proceeding with the project.

Another reason overlooked by the early surveys of the 1850's was identified in the field work of 1906. The engineers reported that because of the number of people now living by the shores of Lake Nipissing, the lake could no longer be flooded to create the reservoir needed for the locks.

But the idea would never die particularly in the minds of many board members. In 1942 another resolution was made to further "explore the connections with Georgian Bay Canal project." On June 9, 1960, "Resolved that the Chamber request the Northern Economic Development Commission proceed with the investigation of the economic feasibility of construction of the ship canal between Georgian Bay and Lake Nipissing more especially at this time when the Department of Public Works in Ottawa have promised to make a survey of the French River at the earliest date possible..., to make a study of a previous report and survey made of the Georgian Bay Canal about 1908." In 1963 and 1965 the Chamber again reiterated their stance, "Chamber endorses and supports the idea of a engineering and economic feasibility study of the Georgian Canal proposal."

As late as 1993 when the new government of Jean Chretien announced billions of dollars for infrastructure projects, the prospects of a recreational waterway resurfaced. Many pleasure boaters are for it, but the French River is designated as a Canadian Heritage River. The "Grand Canal" remains only in the annals of history.

The Ezylife Canoe Club might have been underwater if the Georgian Bay ship canal ever became a reality. Located on Parsons Avenue, it was a popular club for canoeists. Nipissing Archives/North Bay Area Museum photo.

A Lasting Symbol

The historic old stone arch is a landmark. It is immortalized on thousands of postcards, letterheads, crests and souvenirs and is one of the most photographed points of interest in the North Bay area. For years, before North Bay amalgamated with West Ferris in 1968, the familiar gateway arch signalled, "you're home again!"

It is probably the most enduring way to recognize North Bay. The label, "Gateway City" has stuck with us for a long time.

The "Gateway" first appears in Board of Trade member, A.C.(Cecil) Rorabeck's promotional booklet of 1910. In the first sentence it says of North Bay, "As the eastern gateway into newer Ontario, seated on the northern shore of Island Gem'd (sic), Lake Nipissing, being one of the brightest, most prosperous towns in the New Ontario group."

In the 1913-14 version of the same Board publication the first sentences read: "Looking at it from a commercial viewpoint North Bay commands an ideal location. Frequently it has been termed 'The Gateway to the North' - a land vast in its area, which has been proudly referred to by its inhabitants as 'The Rich and Fertile Northland.'

"The Gateway of the North" logo evolved from the arch erected in 1928 at the City's eastern limits. It was an idea put forth by the Associated Canadian Travellers (A.C.T.) to city council in 1928. They contracted North Bayite, Jack Billington to build the arch.

Their fraternal organization of salesmen (originally known as the North Bay Travellers prior to 1934) represented firms doing business in the wholesale and industrial sector of the economy. Serving Northern Ontario from head offices in southern Ontario, North Bay was, geographically, a good place to locate. Members of the North Bay A.C.T. were actively involved in community service.

Eventually as Highway 11/Lakeshore Drive widened, the arch was modified and rededicated in 1960. One of the pillars had to be reconstructed after a truck collision. Finally with the construction of the "overpass" in 1968 the arch was removed and installed in Lee Park and rededicated in its new location in 1975 on the occasion of the Association's Biannual Conference.

In December of 1989 the ACT were outspoken against the city's plan to change North Bay's longstanding logo. Dan Corbeil, chairman of the ACT preservation of our logo committee, said in a Nugget article, "there is no good reason" to change the logo, "it's still a good representation of the community, with its emphasis on air, road and rail services. Why change it? It's still modern-looking. Imagine the cost of putting a new logo on letterhead, city trucks and tool boxes. That will cost a lot more than the $10,000 the city is spending on a new logo." Although the city has a revised logo, the tradition of what was initiated years ago, continues in a refashioned manner and the "Gateway" remains dear to our hearts.

The North Bay Travellers evolved into a chapter of the ACT and they will always be remembered for one of North Bay's most famous landmarks, constructed in 1928. James Kelly collection - Nugget photo.

The World Knows Us

It is not a new story. It is a tale about how five little girls entered the world, and it has been told and retold countless times. The odds were incalculable, as identical quintuplets were developed from a single egg, and they were given little chance to survive.

For some it is a sad story mixing exploitation, manipulation, politics, religion, cultural identity and greed. Their lives have been the subject of many books, films and plays. For years the Dionne Quintuplets have remained out of the public eye, but public interest remains high. For the Board of Trade and later the Chamber of Commerce the Quints have provided the best and most trying of times.

More importantly their birth brought world attention to Corbeil and to the whole Nipissing area, it brought joy to a world weary of the Great Depression.

It's a story that had its beginnings in a little farmhouse near Corbeil (Highway 94), east of Callander on May 28, 1934. On that day Mrs. Elzire Dionne gave birth to the first quintuplets in history to survive infancy. In order of birth the girls were named Yvonne, Annette, Cecile, Emilie and Marie.

First news of the unprecedented birth went by telegram from the office of The Daily Nugget to the Canadian Press (Toronto) after a brother of the father Oliva, Leon Dionne, telephoned The Nugget and jokingly inquired whether or not a birth notice for five would be more expensive than the usual announcement.

The Quintuplets were weighed for the first time on potato scales by William Dumsday, a Nugget reporter, who informed editor Richard Bunyan, that the sensational sisters weighed in at a combined total of 13 pounds, six ounces. The smallest (Marie) weighed slightly more than a pound. At the same time one of the most published photographs in newspaper history appeared in every major newspaper in the world. It is the only picture (taken by R. R. Railton) showing the five babies in bed with their mother on the day of their birth.

The Industry

The Quintuplets brought tourism to life in the North Bay area often drawing 6,000 people a day to their nursery. It was a fenced-in compound containing a guard house, staff house, nursery and public and private play area. What it didn't contain was their parents, brothers and sisters.

"You can cash in on the fact they are in your district," stated Jack Hambleton, the director of the Ontario publicity bureau, telling members of the North Bay Board of Trade in April of 1935. Leo Dolan of the Canadian government tourist bureau told the Board in 1936, the Quints were "the greatest tourist attraction on the face of the globe!" With the co-ordinating efforts of the Board of Trade and the Ontario government, promotional literature laid the grounds for a burgeoning tourist industry.

"Quintland" became the mecca for motoring tourists and pamphlets would highlight the area for years:

"By car, by bus, by train... All roads lead to Callander since the arrival of the Quints! Highway 11 runs straight north from Toronto; Highway 17 brings you from Ottawa, Canada's capital; and from the west, you will come through Sault Ste. Marie and Sudbury over 294 miles of good road. The Canadian National Railway passes right through the town of Callander, and the Canadian Pacific through North Bay, the 'Gateway of the North,' only three miles distant. Each road traverses beautiful country, touches important Canadian cities and towns. And around this most famous nursery in the world lies one of Ontario's loveliest playgrounds, with many comfortable places to stay, both rustic and luxurious...with wonderful fishing, good bathing and boating. The whole family will be happy in Quintland this summer!"

It didn't take the Board long to see the potential of the Quints. In a December 28, 1934 resolution, "That the Board of Trade take immediate action to enlist the co-operation of the guardians of the famous Dionne Quintuplets of Callander, to work in co-operation with our Board of Trade. With the daily publicity throughout Canada and the United States, we will in all probability see thousands of new tourists in Northern Ontario." It was a prophetic statement.

As a result, the tourist trade exploded. In 1936 the Canadian tourist trade reported an 8 per cent increase, North Bay experienced a business upswing of 75 per cent. In the community accommodation was at a premium. Private residences in the city doubled as tourist homes as there was little room for the influx of thousands of visitors.

In 1936 the Star Weekly reported that, "Everyone cashes in on the babies," and that more people had become familiar with Northern Ontario in 24 months than in the preceding 50 years.

In Pierre Berton's book, 'The Dionne Years,' he states: "The Quints saved North Bay from financial disaster. The city, staggering under an annual relief bill of a quarter of a million dollars ran out of funds in June of 1936 and was unable to persuade the provincial government to bail it out. In order to meet relief payments, it was forced to dip into its reserve fund for uncollected taxes, an action that caused Roy Thomson (future Lord Thomson of Fleet) to resign as alderman."

In a 1935 Board of Trade report it states, "Our manager satisfactorily handles 4,262 visitors in 92 days, an increase of 60 percent over the previous year. The prospects for this year are even greater owing to the fact the Dionne Quintuplets will bring thousands of tourists to the North Bay district."

Manipulation and Money

Two months after the Quints' birth the Ontario government appointed a board of guardians to protect the health and interests of the girls, effectively stripping control from their parents.

In the Quintuplets version of what happened, ('We Were Five' by James Brough), they said, "Dad and Mom did not appear at the North Bay court house on the appointed day to sign their assent to our being placed in the board's custody. To show their disapproval of the whole proceeding, they stayed away. It was the first of many similar absences, not forgetting our own first birthday party."

Dr. Dafoe, W.H. Anderson of the Red Cross Society and Kenneth Morrisson, a Callander merchant (and friend of Dafoe), and the Quints' grandfather were appointed guardians by the government. Since he was responsible for their health he was given near control over the Quintuplets.

Dr. Dafoe directed all aspects of the Quints early childhood development. While the parents were allowed to visit the children, they were left out of the decisions relating to how their daughters should be raised. It was the start of a battle between father and doctor that lasted until February 14, 1941 when the government removed Dr. Dafoe and restored custody of the Quints to the Dionnes.

As the battle over endorsements, custody and control continued for the Quintuplets, The Nugget in a May 16, 1941 editorial said, "All parties concerned should get together to make sure that the Quintuplet picture is such that it will draw a maximum of visitors from the United States..."

A Legacy

In 1985 the Chamber of Commerce helped purchase the Dionne homestead, but the project was not without controversy. One hundred thousand dollars was raised by the Dionne Patrons Foundation to purchase the small, two-storey frame structure. It was moved from its former site adjacent to the Pinewood Park Motor Inn to the present regional tourist information centre.

The Dionne Quints resurfaced in 1993 through legal representation. They laid claim to a portion of the profits generated from the museum operated by the Chamber.

A strong memory remains in the minds of hundreds of thousands of persons all over the world - a memory of five babies who brought the charm of a miracle to a generation who lived through the cynical era of the Great Depression and the sadness of World War II.

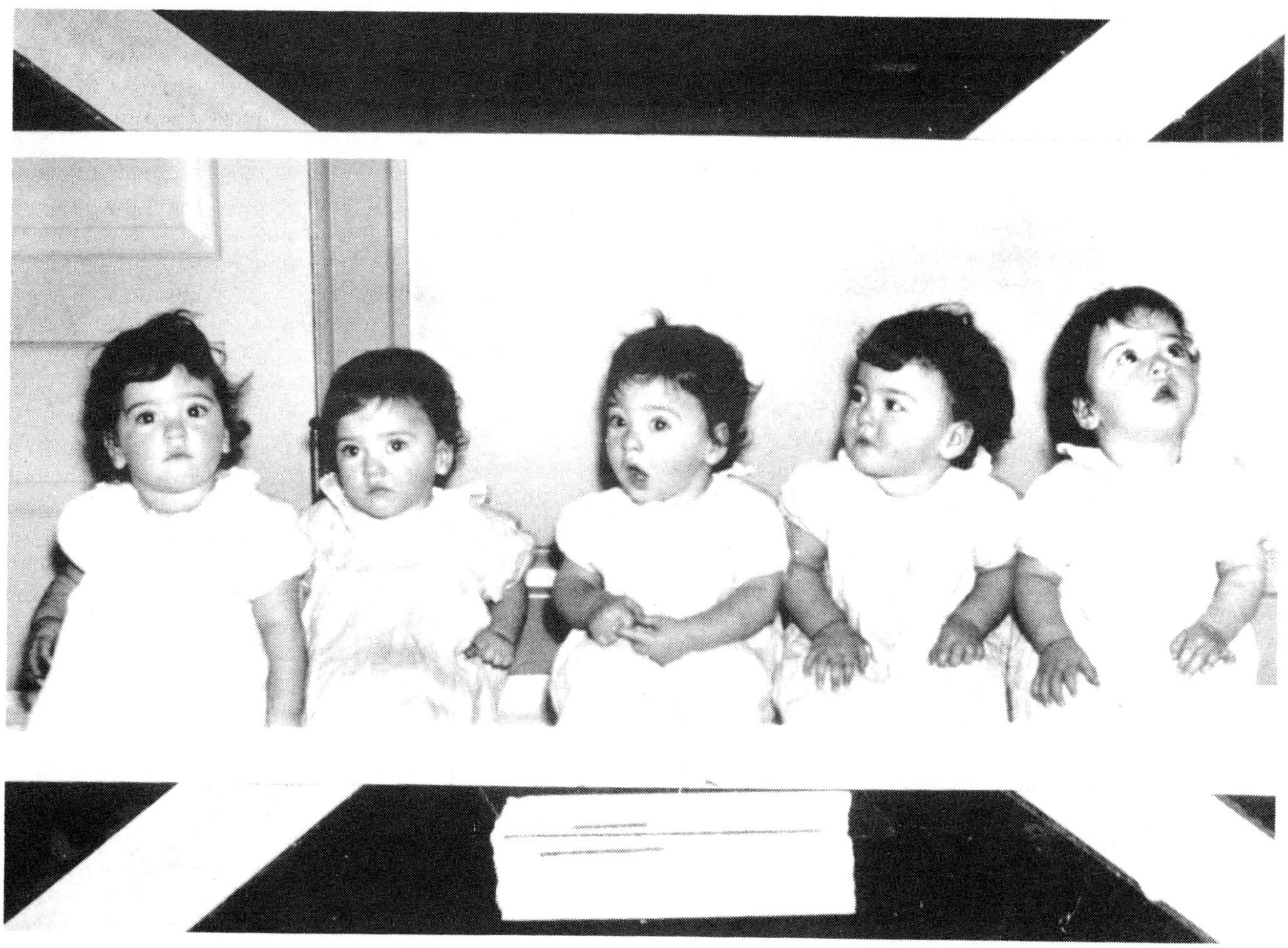

The World Famous Dionne Quintuplets; Yvonne, Annette, Cecile, Emilie and Marie. Dionne Quints Museum collection, original copyright NEA Inc.

Highway Taps Payroll

It is still a windy highway but it is the only link from North Bay to Temiscaming.

The "model company town" developed by C.B. Thorne was without a highway to the outside world. A campaign by the Board of Trade culminated on September 6, 1937 when Mitchell Hepburn, premier of Ontario opened the North Bay-Temiscaming highway (Highway 63). Previous access to the area was only possible by a CPR spur line from Mattawa. Residents of the community often said that when the daily train left the station the only way to the outside world was to walk.

From its humble beginnings as a sawmill town it developed from a 1918 plan to include a bleached sulphite mill, a control dam at the foot of Lake Temiskaming, and emerged as a formidable company town. After various difficulties the mill and town were taken over by the Canadian International Paper Company in 1925.

The importance of reaching this community was outlined in a Janurary 23, 1933 Nugget article. "The town of Temiskaming, (earlier spelling used at the time) where the Canadian International Paper Company operates a large plant is one of the most flourishing industrial centres in the north. Proof of Temiskaming's importance from an industrial standpoint is given in the fact that the sustaining plant contributed in the past fiscal year, one per cent of the total excise duties collected by the Dominion government. This indicates the enormity of the company's operations and the town's position in an industrial sense."

The Board of Trade with the North Bay Unemployed Association and the mayors of North Bay, Mattawa and Temiskaming formed a delegation to interview George Henry, Premier of Ontario. The Great Depression had hit the northland and road construction created work camps for hundreds of men. At the same time a trunk road from Mattawa joining the North Bay-Temiscaming road (now Highway 533) was included in their discussions.

With a monthly company payroll of $45,000, merchants in North Bay saw the highway as one way to increase sales. The road was also identified for "exceptional areas of settlement," and one that "possesses immeasureable wealth from the point of the view of the sportsman and tourist," (Nugget article). There were more than 40,000 people living in northwestern Quebec (Ville Marie, Rouyn, Noranda and Amos) who had no outlet to Ontario and eastern Canada.

Nugget reporter, Britt Jessup recalls accompanying three Board of Trade members, Jack Hall and Clare Beattie, and Les Banner, "a real booster of the highway," on a trip during construction of the highway. "We stopped at the construction camps along the way and chatted with the various foremen of the different gangs. Finally we reached the spot where it was no longer possible to drive.

"Clearing and stumping was proceeding, but it would be many weeks before one could drive right through. So we set out afoot, and after a walk of about three miles, came to the bridge which joined Ontario and Quebec.

"There, waiting for us with a small reception committee comprised of town officials, was Mayor Allan K. Grimmer of Temiskaming. He had somehow gotten word of our adventure, and decided to greet us.

"Mayor Grimmer was a wonderful host. He took us to his lovely home, and it was there that I had my first martini. Interest was keen as both communities eagerly awaited the first highway linking North Bay and Temiskaming. Then, it was on to the White Oaks Inn, where he had arranged a small banquet. The food was delicious, and so was the wine. After a good night's sleep it was back to the trail and eventually to our car. For a young reporter it was a real story."

With much fanfare the road was officially opened on Labour Day Monday, 1937 on the island in the middle of the Ottawa River. Premier Mitchell Hepburn of Ontario untied "green and white ribbons" and a stone cairn was unveiled to commemorate the event.

Much credit was given to the Board of Trade during the ceremony. Mayor Robert Rowe of North Bay paid tribute to Board of Trade members, A.H. Kilgour, "who first envisioned the road and its possibilities," and J.H. MacDonald, E.L. Banner, T.J. Patton and D.G. Stevens. From 1920 when the Board of Trade was contacted by the Town of Temiskaming to the early 1930's the idea was continually "boosted" in the provincial legislature.

During the years prior to the opening of the highway, interchanges between the two communities were organized. Special excursions by rail between North Bay and Temiskaming were arranged. This day had been a long time coming and many Temiskaming residents couldn't wait. It was not uncommon for people to walk as far as 14 kilometres from the Ontario/Quebec border to the end of the road construction in order to hitch a ride along the new route and spend a few hours living and enjoying the sights of a city.

W.G. Bulbrook, ex-mayor of North Bay told the audience that with so many highways and railroads already in existence he at first opposed the building of the highway, but that he had been "converted to the project." He congratulated the North Bay Board of Trade for its efforts in having the road built.

Mayor A.K. Grimmer, of Temiskaming said, "We of Temiskaming have waited many years for this day." And the town was never quite the same again.

Persuasion Brings Power

Electrical power is a fundamental form of energy in our society. The indispensable importance to our lives is most obvious when you walk into a darkened room and reach for the light switch.

For early residents of North Bay it wasn't so easy. On a number of occasions the Board of Trade can be thanked for bringing power to the people. It may have been self serving for the business community, but community leaders have always recognized it to be an expensive proposition.

In the late 1880's electricity was introduced to the fledgling community of pioneers by private enterprise and in the true spirit of business there evolved a rivalry between steam and water generated power.

The first settlers to North Bay came in 1882 because of the national vision of an east-west railway uniting all of Canada. Wood and coal fired their stoves, furnaces and oil lamps provided light. There was no electricity.

John Bourke arrived in 1885 and built a steam-engine driven sawmill which turned out lumber needed for the rapidly developing settlement. There is evidence that Mr. Bourke possessed a small electric dynamo (generator) that was used to supply electric lighting for his own enterprises.

In 1892 the Royal Electric Company of Toronto approached town council to establish an electric lighting service in the community. But with little money no action was taken on the initiative.

Mr. Bourke had become the first mayor of the inaugurated town (April 7, 1890) and had erected two mills in the west end of town. There remains a concrete foundation of the mill at the end of Nipissing St.

By 1894 Mr. Bourke was no longer the mayor and he had persuaded council to give him a 10-year franchise to supply residents with electricity from his generating plant.

In Barney Graham's book, 'North Bay Hydro 1885-1973,' he states, "During the daylight hours the steam engine (fueled by coal) was driving the saws and planers but then at dusk when the day's work was over the drive belt was slipped off of the saw drive and put on the pulley of the dynamo. The old steam engine had to do double duty and drive the generator until midnight when the service was shut down." The original installation was crude by today's standards but the service did provide lighting for many homes.

One of North Bay's prominent families was the John Bourke family. This was the 1901 wedding of Anne Elizabeth Bourke, eldest daughter of John, to Henry McDonnell a railway mail clerk. Sandra Stinson family collection.

It was at this time that the newly created Board of Trade started to petition council regarding street lighting. The reason becomes evident in the extensive promotional booklet published by the Board of Trade in 1895. To be considered a progressive town various utilites had to be part of infrastructure development. It was a drawing card to businesses and families looking for new municipalities.

With the backing of the Board of Trade, Mr. Bourke turned his attention to convincing the politicians of the day to light their streets. The Board of Trade sent several pieces of correspondence regarding the matter and these are recorded in the early records of council minutes.

In September of 1898 Mr. Bourke received a contract for the installation of 15 lighting standards, one on Oak St., seven on Main St., five on McIntyre St and two on Worthington St. There was not much more to the downtown and the residential sections of what was a small town. It was an expensive proposition as the lamps had to be started each evening by a night constable. And in the true spirit of conservation the lighting system was shut down on full, moonlight nights. The ornamental light standards that now beautify the downtown core are representative of what these lights would have been like.

In 1904, Mr. Bourke's plant was bought out by the newly formed North Bay Light, Heat and Power Co., with Mr. Bourke as a director. By this time the Temiskaming and Northern Ontario Railway had arrived in North Bay and there was now a V.O.N. Hospital on Klock Ave (Algonquin Ave.). The town was growing and the private utility changed its service from direct to alternating current which was a major step in providing continuous service that had more flexibility in installation use.

But all was not well. There was considerable dissatifaction with the steam-generated service provided by the private utility and numerous complaints were lodged by and through the Board of Trade to council. So much so the town corresponded with the provincial government on the possibility of developing a hydro (water) installation at the Chaudiere Falls on the French River. Nothing came of this proposal, but it is important to realize that the technology of harnessing water power was becoming a reality. In Southern Ontario it had become a political issue. Hydro power was unique at its inception, and the visions of Sir Adam Beck - inexpensive electricity owned by the people was a popular notion for all municipalities, including North Bay.

A Toronto-based company, the Nipissing Power Co., had started (1907) work on a generating station at the McNabb Chutes on the South River, just outside the village of Nipissing. The same company had begun negotiations with North Bay to change the steam-powered water

It was all manpower when utility poles were needed. The rocky nature of the city is also indicated, circa 1912. Nipissing Archives/North Bay Area Museum.

pumps taking water from Lake Nipissing. It was during 1905-07 that the North Bay Light, Heat and Power Co., had endeavoured to establish a much longer term of 30 years. The Board of Trade continued to pressure council to make a decision. Both companies were heard by council on matters of rates, service and contracts. No firm commitment was made by council and the rivalry continued, both trying to make money for their stockholders.

In 1908 the town proposed to takeover the North Bay, Light, Heat and Power Co. - the price to be fixed by arbitration and paid for in municipal bonds over a period of 30 years at an interest rate of four and one-half percent. Put to a municipal vote it was rejected by town citizens. At the same time the plans of the Nipissing Power Co., continued. By 1910 a single transmission line had made its way from the power generating station on the South River to the hydro substation on Worthington St, near John St.

During the period of 1910-1912, North Bay was partially powered by steam generated electricity and hydro electricity. In 1912, the Nipissing Power Co. bought out its rival and became the sole private utility until 1916 when the recently formed Hydro Electric Power

Jobs were plentiful and machines were scarce in 1922 as many men help unload utility poles. Nipissing Archives/North Bay Area Museum photo.

Commission (Ontario Hydro) took over the distribution system for the province. It was the end of private profitmaking, power was now produced at cost.

In 1922 the issue of a town-owned electric power distribution plant came before council again, but no positive action was taken on the proposal. It would be another ten years before a concerted effort was made by the Board of Trade to have North Bay secure a municipally owned utility. Many articles in The Nugget and presentations to council brought some action. The Board said in their promotional literature, "When power can be supplied at reasonable cost, there will be opportunities for the larger interests which they cannot afford to overlook."

North Bay was built on rock and this photo, in the early 1920's, indicates the hand labour required to install this pole mount. Nipissing Archives/North Bay Area Museum photo.

In 1932 a city council resolution was passed acknowledging that negotiations with Ontario Electric Power Commission should begin. There was continual pressure to reduce the high rates charged by the provincial utility.

Faced with the continued impossibility of being able to offer industries, considering establishing themselves in North Bay, a power rate comparable with that of other Ontario cities the Board of Trade continued to examine the issue. Late in 1939, four members of the Board's executive, including President Walter Little were added to a committee established by the Board to examine the possibility of the municipality taking over the power system. The Board continued to examine what inducements could be offered to industries with a municipally owned utility.

By the next year city bylaws were designed and the matter was submitted to ratepayers for a vote on May 10, 1940. It was approved by them 663 in favour, 413 against. The actual transfer cost of the distribution system was $228,769.33. With the support of the electorate North Bay was now managing its own utility. It was good news in a 1945 advertisement, "...For the fourth time since that decision was made North Bay hydro rates have been reduced. Once again the claims of those who said that the purchase of the distribution system from the Ontario Hydro Electric Power Commission would, among other things, result in lower rates, have been vindicated. On Thursday, the North Bay commission announced rate reductions resulting from five to 20 percent...For many years prohibitive power rates did much to discourage new industries from coming to this city, but, fortunately, that obstacle has now been removed and every effort should be made to capitalize on this favourable situation."

With a North Bay managed utility and lower rates industries did arrive, including Craig Bit in 1941 and a large expansion to Longyear in 1947.

A pole was all that was needed for members of the Ezylife Canoe Club to have a little fun in the 1920's. Nipissing Archives/North Bay Area Museum photo.

A Nugget Of News

We owe a great deal to our community newspapers. They remain the permanent record of growth and development, of births and deaths, of local and global news. The newspaper is a vital link in community services.

Organizations such as the Board of Trade/Chamber of Commerce have used this medium to make changes in the community through news events and advertising. The newspaper was an important vehicle to "boost" North Bay proposals at various levels of government. In many cases, with strong support by The Nugget, the Board/Chamber has been able to convince municipal council of the adage, "what was good for business was best for the community."

An Important Day

On Saturday, March 1, 1941 The Nugget - the North's leading newspaper - became a daily.

Noting this prestigious day and the importance of the newspaper in North Bay was a letter from the Board of Trade featured on the front page (second section) on the first daily run. It was a fitting tribute authored by President D.G. Stevens. "Your faith in this district and its possibilities is clearly indicated in making this important decision. As a daily edition, your paper will be a real service to this community and the whole of Northern Ontario, which you have so faithfully served for many years as a tri-weekly." There is little doubt The Nugget also recognized the important contributions of the Board of Trade, for it is rare that letters are featured on the front page of any newspaper.

It was owned by Board of Trade member, W.E. Mason who served as president and publisher of the newspaper. Mr. Mason owned the old Pacific Hotel, (St. Regis) and at the time of its going daily ran both the paper and hotel out of the same building. The new daily was to cost its readers three cents a delivered copy.

The Nugget was born in 1906 in North Bay where it was printed and then shipped to Cobalt, the silver and boom capital of Northern Ontario. At the time it was known as the only newspaper in Canada to have such a distinctive name, it was a natural for a mining town newspaper. It was the start of one of the oldest, established newspapers in the north. The Nugget used the first roll of newsprint turned out at the mill of the Abitibi Power and Paper Company at Iroquois Falls. It was also the first Northern Ontario newspaper to carry Canadian Press news to its readers.

Eventually a newspaper plant in Cobalt was built and was issued continuously as a weekly newspaper until January of 1909 when it became a daily known as the Cobalt Daily Nugget.

By 1922 the mining boom was over and it was moved back to North Bay. In the same year Mr. Mason purchased the newspaper and during the next 19 years functioned as a tri-weekly until reaching daily status in 1941. Following the death of Mr. Mason a group of five employees - Jack F. Grainger, Mort Fellman, Britt Jessup, George Justice and Jack Beatty were able to purchase the newspaper from the estate. It was a promise fulfilled by Mr. Mason. In the mid-fifties the employee-owned newspaper was purchased by its present owner, Southam Incorporated.

Outstanding Contribution

For many years the Chamber's monthly Board of Directors meetings have been open to the public. Local news media representatives from The Nugget, CFCH-CKAT, MCTV and CHUR are usually in attendance.

Chamber meetings and events were covered for The Nugget for more than 20 years by Betty Alcorn who was news editor when she died in 1977 at the age of 52. So outstanding was her contribution to the Chamber over the years that she was presented with a special award by the Ontario Chamber of Commerce in Toronto in 1974. In her memory the Chamber instituted the Betty Alcorn Memorial Award in 1978. This award is presented annually to a member of the Chamber's Board of Directors voted by his/her peers as having best exemplified dedication and diligence and having laboured untiringly for the good and welfare of the Chamber and the community. Past winners are: Gary Pluim, Rosemary Zelinka, George Lowe, Romeo Messier, Ed O'Hagan, Henry Drenth, George Maroosis, Chuck Kelly, Victor Fedeli, Gary Jodouin, Rick Evans, Amir Jaffer, Jim Colyer, Glenn Edmonds, Barry Spilchuk, Stella Colyer, Anthony Rota, Judy Duchesne, Jack Campbell and Jeff Rogerson.

Working with the Community

The relationship between The Nugget and the Chamber of Commerce is best summarized in an editorial written on the 80th anniversary of the Chamber in 1974.

"A happy relationship based on mutual support has applied through the years between the North Bay and District Chamber of Commerce and The Nugget."

"The reason, of course, is that both have an involvement in a common cause: the 'general betterment' of North Bay and the men, women and children who live here."

"...Since any purpose that involves general betterment of a city and its people touches on any and all facets of the community, there is really no end to the list of shared projects that have been undertaken by the Chamber and The Nugget in the past, or will be, in the future."

The late Hartley Trussler who wrote a regular column in The Nugget entitled 'Reflections' wrote on March 29, 1974, "Considering what the Chamber of Commerce has done over the years it truly can be said, 'If the Chamber didn't do it, who would?' It has a proud record of achievements."

She wasn't the Queen then, but Princess Elizabeth paid a visit to North Bay in 1951. Nipissing Archives/North Bay Area Museum photo.

Before The Nugget came the "North Bay Times" and the town in 1890 was a pioneer community. Nipissing Archives/North Bay Area Museum photo.

Water, Water Everywhere

Every spring the level of Lake Nipissing comes under close scrutiny. Throughout the past severe floods affecting the North Bay shoreline and the neighbourhoods bordering Chippewa Creek have been recorded.

Public outcry is the voice that has prompted the Board of Trade and Chamber of Commerce to listen to and act upon fluctuating water levels.

It wasn't until 1907 that the level of Lake Nipissing was controlled by man. In that year two log crib dams were built. But by 1909 the dams were being ravaged by ice jams and were already in a state of disrepair. This made flood conditions on the lake only worse. One area resident said in 1909, "I can remember paddling my canoe through the door of the flooded Hudson Bay Trading Post (in Sturgeon Falls)."

In 1916 the Big Chaudiere Dam was completed. It was started before the war by federal funds as part of a "mega" project that proposed connecting Lake Nipissing and Georgian Bay. With its steel gates it controlled the outflow through two natural channels. The construction was significant for the North Bay Board of Trade as it kept the "Grand Canal" scheme alive.

By 1919 the 'French River Improvement,' endorsed by The Associated Boards of Trade of Ontario, was being bantered about by federal and provincial politicians. It included the Georgian Bay Canal scheme which would make North Bay an eastern grain terminal, a deep water port served by three railways.

The construction of this permanent dam was seen as the beginning of a plan often compared to the Panama Canal in terms of its magnitude. But further construction and implementation of the entire project would never take place, although efforts to make it a reality would continue for decades.

(The Board of Trade also pushed and was successful in having the winged breakwater constructed at the end of the government dock. On August, 21, 1931, a resolution states: "That whereas the harbor at North Bay has no protection from the high seas caused by south or westerly winds, and whereas the use of small craft has been abandoned through boats being destroyed while at their mooring at the dock, therefore be it resolved that this Board petition the Federal Government to have a suitable break-water erected a this point.")

Although the dams constructed helped, major floods hit the North Bay shoreline in 1928, 1933, 1947 and 1960.

From early minutes of the Board it is recorded in a resolution (April 21, 1932), "that in view

Floods have been a problem for the North Bay shoreline. This shot in 1920 shows the high water level at the Government Dock. Nipissing Archives/North Bay Area Museum photo.

of the exceptionally high level of Lake Nipissing water that Public Works Department at Ottawa be queried as to the condition of gates at French River and that Department be asked to furnish this Board with statement of high and low levels each month."

Another strong warning of impending disaster was issued on October 18, 1945. "Whereas the water level of Lake Nipissing is a matter of concern to hundreds of permanent home owners, and to other lakeshore residents, and whereas at several periods during every year the high water level of the lake is the cause of anxiety and anguish to those who have investments in shore-line properties, and whereas it is evident that present facilities are inadequate to properly take care of this problem, be it resolved that the Federal and Provincial governments be again reminded that the building of a suitable spillway should be undertaken as soon as possible."

It was after the 1947 flood that the Board of Trade made the dams an immediate concern. From May 26 to the peak on June 27 water was four feet deep (1.2 m) on Sunset Boulevard and came close to Lakeshore Drive. On May 26 and 27, high winds caused considerable damage, many cottages had their foundations washed away by high waves. The waves were so high they were reported to have hit the windows of cabins set well back from the lakeshore. Chippewa Creek overflowed, several streets were under water, including Monk St., Second Ave. and McIntyre St. East. During this flood there was no organized sandbagging, therefore damage was extensive. Basements, furnaces, coal and wood supplies suffered the most damage. As a result tourist resorts opened late that season. Some could not open until July 19 and others until August 1.

Due to high water, erosion became a problem for the Lakeshore Hotel at Amelia Park in 1914. Nipissing Archives/North Bay Area Museum photo.

In an August 21 resolution of the flood year, action was taken by the Chamber, "That Leo Gauthier (M.P.) be requested to arrange an appointment with the Federal Minister of Public Works to meet a delegation from this Board, which will urge that a survey of the Lower French be made immediately in the hope that, if feasible, work on a spillway to control the level of Lake Nipissing may be undertaken before the spring of 1948."

It was followed by a November 1948 resolution: "That the North Bay Chamber of Commerce investigate the authority for the control of the dams on the French River with a view to determining what represents normal lake level and how this is determined. Also to make every effort to establish through the proper authorities, what action is necessary to have the dams opened immediately so that the water level of Lake Nipissing will be brought down to such an extent that the threat of high water in the spring will be eliminated."

Action was taken and what was to become the Portage Dam was completed by Public Works in 1950. The man-made sluiceway and stop-log dam was primarily used to draw the lake down to a lower level. Its retaining sill is lower than the Big and Little Chaudiere Dams. Today modern technology brings automation to the operation of the Big Chaudiere Dam. The steel gates can be controlled by desktop computer. Refurbishment of the dams has also taken place.

It is interesting to note that the November 1948 resolution pointed to a control and a responsibility problem that involved not just the Chaudiere dams. Ontario Hydro, Ministry of Natural Resources, Public Works and MacMillan Bloedel all operate dams that control water entering Lake Nipissing. With the assistance of the Chamber of Commerce, municipalities, tourist operators and other interest groups organized in 1980.

Fluctuating water levels continued to occur and the creation of a plan designed by the Sturgeon River/Lake Nipissing/French River Watershed Management Advisory Board has helped. The plan outlines the various responsibilities of government organizations and the private sector that operate dams on watersheds entering Lake Nipissing.

Nature plays a major role in the problem of water level management. A very shallow lake, influenced by westerly winds and one outflow draining several watersheds, with varying amounts of precipitation compound the spring freshet. The building of dams was inevitable, but without the pressing need for permanent dams, flood damage would have been much higher than what has already been experienced.

Waterfront Showcase

It was a long time coming. The development of North Bay's waterfront was the progressive thinking of a group of people with the motivation supplied by the Board/Chamber.

Minutes from the Board reveal that by the end of 1923 it was recommended to town council that it establish a parks/planning commission to look at the future of development within North Bay. There was a great deal of concern amongst members about planning for the continuous and orderly development of the city.

North Bay City Council appointed a town planning commission, November 11, 1926 (it was called town planning even though North Bay had become a city in 1925). One member was J.W. Richardson who had been Board of Trade president in 1920 and 1921.

Under the direction of the planning commission a Toronto firm of consulting engineers, and architects, Bunnell & Borgstrom Limited were engaged to study future prospects in terms of development.

The 1927 report recommended the obtaining of land for recreational purposes along the waterfront, primarily from Duchesnay Creek to the present government wharf. In 1927 the Temiskaming & Northern Ontario Railway donated 28 acres for what was to become Lee Park, the only area officially designated to parks. Little did the consultants of 1927 realize that a man-made connection would someday be made to establish a continuous waterfront.

The report also bemoaned the fact that railway tracks were found throughout developed portions of the city. And it offered the opinion that it was regrettable that all the railways were not kept together in one area of the city. "Despite the fact that North Bay is located on one of the largest and most fascinating inland lakes in Canada the waterfront across the entire extent of the City is in private hands and is most unattractive."

With a view of what would take decades and remains unaccomplished: "With further reference to Park Development on the lakefront, it is our definite recommendation that negotiations be entered into at once with the Canadian Pacific Railway."

It was not until the 1965 that the Chamber of Commerce considered bringing public attention to the development of the waterfront. In a September resolution the chamber stated it would notify "City Council, Minister of Municipal Affairs and C.P. Railway that they would like to see the lakeshore properties owned by the C.P.R. developed with consideration to general public recreation and tourist potential." It was the start of a campaign that would set the wheels in motion for action on the lakeshore.

The Government Dock in 1907, note the original sandy shoreline. In the background is the original indoor skating rink and the North Bay Tennis Club. Nipissing Archives/North Bay Area Museum photo.

It wasn't the wild west but the stockyards were a familiar sight on North Bay's waterfront at the turn of the century. Nipissing Archives/North Bay Area Museum photo.

In 1978 the Chamber took more action. Land covering 120,000 square feet was recovered from previous industrial and railway use and turned into a small park and beach with a change house. Chairman of the Chamber's lakefront development committee, Jack Page, described how three years of negotiations with the federal department of transport and Marathon Realty (CPR) resulted in a lease agreement to develop the land. "The Chamber is taking a largely forgotten section of shoreline and turning it into a public recreational area for use by residents and tourists." It was the start of things to come and as Mr. Page said, "the start of giving the shores of Lake Nipissing back to the people." And the Chamber did give it back. Work parties helped turn the long-forgotten into an attractive parkette. Chamber members loaned heavy equipment to move tons of debris, brush and steel. One idea to raise funds was to charge lake users for parking spaces. Past President, James McGinn along with lakefront development committee members, Daphne Mayne, George Lowe and Bunty Swanson were very involved in the progressive changes of the waterfront.

Within the next decade more talk resulted in action. In April of 1979 the long awaited railway relocation study was released. One of the goals of the land use plan and its development controls was "to provide improved public access to and a variety of development opportunities on the waterfront." Under the land use context the study identified that "due to the location of the CPR line and yards, downtown North Bay is separated from the waterfront; the waterfront has never been able to become part of the city." It also points out the downtown area "is in danger of future decline if the diversity of commercial, retail and entertainment facilities is not enhanced."

What evolved was a multi-phased plan resulting in the opening of the waterfront in 1987. It is an area that reflects civic pride. Much of the man-made waterfront was backfilled with rock taken from the original SAGE underground development of National Defence. It was decided the proposed waterfront plan should not depend on rail relocation because the "railway has no plans for relocating in the foreseeable future (1983)."

Many leaders in the community had the foresight to know that the city would grow and the knowledge that plans should be designed for a logical, economical and orderly development of the city. This is often not enough to ensure that this type of logical development is followed, but it is interesting to note that with the waterfront some of the suggestions were eventually followed producing a landscape that showcases our community.

Crossroads Development

In recent years, there has been a continued call for the four-laning of Highways 11, 17 and 69. In 1994 with the new Liberal government's infrastructure scheme there has been renewed interest in highway construction in the northland. The transportation links with Southern Ontario and the rest of Canada have always been important to the development of the "Gateway City."

Many municipalities, tourist organizations and chambers of commerce are voicing their opinions for improving the highway network. It has become a competition between North Bay and Sudbury to see if Highway 11 or 69 will receive a major boost in highway construction.

A look at an Ontario road map will identify the few highways that penetrate the vast expanse of Northern Ontario. You will notice that Highways 11-north and 17-west both leave North Bay and arrive in Nipigon, both carry the Trans Canada Highway designation. Most of these roads came into existence during the 1920's and 30's. Much of the political debate and lobbying involved the Board of Trade.

The Need

After World War I there was a rapid rise in road traffic that forced the provinces to build their own network of roads. With this in mind, the Ontario government sought to construct the Ferguson Highway (Highway 11-North), from North Bay to give northeastern Ontario a route to the south. The Board of Trade saw itself as a leader in the development of a parallel highway to the T&NO Railway. The North Bay Board of Trade led the way in coordinating other boards in Northern Ontario in their efforts to convince politicians it was a needed project. The highway would be good for local merchants and industry wanting to be close to the natural resources of the northland. In December of 1924 the Board continued to pressure the Government of Ontario. "Before a final survey is made that the matter of diverting the North Bay-Cobalt Highway entrance into North Bay be made in order to avoid Thibeault Hill." They didn't quite get their wish and in 1994 the government is still improving this piece of the highway.

Named after former Premier G. Howard Ferguson, a major force in the planning of the project, the gravel road was a travelling feat in itself. An early motorist venturing north was required to check-in at a booth and gate located near what is now the North Bay Psychiatric

It was a "test" for early motorists. The Ferguson Highway (Highway 11 North) helped promote early travel and tourism in Northeastern Ontario. Nipissing Archives/North Bay Area Museum photo.

The first "lookout" was at the top of Thibeault Hill. Nipissing Archives/North Bay Area Museum photo.

Hospital. The check-in lasted for more than 10 years. In 1925 it was reported that a car got stuck in a soft spot and disappeared in the muskeg near Jumping Caribou Lake. During the early years the road was closed during the winter. Travelling was precarious and a 1927 calvacade of 300 cars travelled north from Toronto for an official opening of the highway. But the rough road took its toll of vehicles and the highway did not receive rave reviews.

In July of 1928, northern road problems in general and the Ferguson highway in particular formed the chief topic of discussion at the quarterly meeting of the Associated Boards of Trade in Haileybury. Delegates heard the highway described as the "impassable morass," a common description of the road after a rainfall. Board representatives wanted the highway put in "permanent shape." At the same meeting, Lands and Forests Minister, Frank Findlayson said, "his hand was forced by this (Associated Boards of Trade) same body." Mr. Findlayson said that by complaining the highway was receiving a "black eye," and "as you people seem to want to do." The Associated Boards of Trade issued a resolution that suggested "that the government would be well advised to discontinue the distribution of folders describing the Ferguson highway as a 'splendid road for motor travel from Severn Bridge to Cochrane' and also that 'on it one may travel easily and comfortably over an improved gravel road.'" Their resolution included the following description, "at its best in real dry weather the road is rough, narrow and dangerously ditched." It would take another 25 years of continuous upgrading, and asphalt paving, to make the road worth travelling. It was renamed the King's Highway 11 in 1936.

East-West.

Recognizing the economic, cultural and social advantages offered by a trans-Canada route, the federal government passed the Canada Highway Act in 1919, under which grants were given to the provinces for province-to-province links. Work started in the 1920's to link Ottawa and North Bay with a route westward. The choice to extend the highway west became a political issue throughout the decade.

Then came The Depression. The Unemployment Relief Act gave work to thousands of men in work camps along the route of the proposed Trans Canada Highway. In a Nugget editorial in the spring of 1931 it stated: "Here at last is one instance of good come of bad. Had it not been for The Depression and the need of providing home and necessities of life, the highway would be a thing of the distant future." Articles from 1929 to 1934 describe the slow, but steady progress of road construction from Pembroke to Mattawa and on to North Bay. Complicating the construction were the constant interruptions of work because of deferred

Construction of the Trans Canada Highway near Rutherglen in 1934. Horse and wagon was the mainstay of construction. Nipissing Archives/North Bay Area Museum photo.

relief payments to the provinces by the federal government. Because the payments were distributed throughout Northern Ontario, many small projects were undertaken, including new unsurfaced roads from Mattawa (Highway 533) to Highway 63, one from Sturgeon Falls to Field and north to Marten River (Highway 64) and the paving of the highway between Callander, Powassan and Sundridge was completed.

In an article taken from the July 7, 1931, edition of The Nugget, an important meeting of the Associated Boards of Northern Ontario was set for North Bay to discuss the link with the Manitoba border. It was a meeting the North Bay Board of Trade had been wanting for a long time as the Gateway City would certainly benefit from the eventual road construction. It was a meeting that would have a long-lasting effect on the landscape of Northern Ontario. What resulted was not a decision at all.

What evolved from the multitude of municipal concerns was the proposal of four routes across the northland. All delegates agreed that the road should be built from North Bay, but from there no consensus was reached. The routes included the costly north of Sault Ste. Marie route along Lake Superior, known as the southern route; the economically feasible and shorter northern route from Hearst; the compromise route following the Canadian Pacific Railway through Chapleau; and another route from Hearst to Sault Ste. Marie that would have a westward junction somewhere between the two communities.

The recommendations forced the federal and provincial governments to undertake more aerial surveys before money could be delegated to the mammoth highway project. Compounding the problem were statements by Prime Minister R.B. Bennett and Premier George S. Henry that they would not announce any decision on any route in the near future.

A Nugget editorial explained the complexity of political football that was coming to an apparent head. "In view of the conflicting claims, the situation politically requires the wisdom of a Solomon, and if Premiers Henry and Bennett can come to a conclusion that will meet sectional ambitions, they will have achieved a unique triumph of diplomacy." Clearly a decision was needed, but none was made.

In an August, 1931 Nugget article the situation was so confusing that a positive side seemed to emerge through the following headline: 'Arguement Over The Route Of Highway Advertises Ontario - Has Been Bitterest Fight In History of the North.' The lead paragraph likened the conflict with the ongoing hockey rivalry experienced between Northern Ontario towns. "Municipal officials, boards of trade, newspaper editors and various other 'defenders of the public' are awaiting eagerly the pronouncement that will decide the fortunes of scores of schemes that have been devised as bait for the government in selecting a location for what will be the longest and most expensive link, with the most problematical advantages to the country as a whole, in the entire trans-Canada road system."

Road construction on all proposed routes including trunk roads (that would become secondary highways) continued throughout the 1930's and was interrupted by World War II. By 1944 it was possible to drive the northern route to Port Arthur (Thunder Bay), but Northwestern Ontario drivers were more likely to put their cars on board a ferry from the Lakehead to the "Soo" and then drive south through Michigan to southern Ontario.

Road construction continued throughout the North, but it was not until the passing of the Trans-Canada Highway Act in 1949 that a decison was made to start the north shore route (Agawa Bay to Marathon) for tourist traffic. The 265-kilometre section through Cambrian granite and heavy forest proved to be a formidable opponent. More than $40-million and 25 bridges were needed to complete the section known as the "The Gap" finished at Wawa in 1960.

The completion of all these roads opened the North to the burgeoning trucking industry needed in resource extraction and the service sector. At the same time tourism became an industry and access became a priority to appreciate our natural amenities.

This is one reason the present Chamber of Commerce continues to push for the four-laning of Highway 11. The completion of the project from Huntsville to North Bay and northwards would again help the Near North become an important travel destination. Which route, Highway 69 or 11, will receive preference may be decided in good time, with a process echoing the past.

You had to be self sufficient when you journeyed outside of North Bay, the roads were rough and the next service station might be in the next community (1920's). Nipissing Archives/ North Bay Area Museum photos.

Before public transportation, Deluxe Coach Lines owned by the Palangio family was a mainstay in the community, photo circa 1940. Nipissing Archives/North Bay Area Museum photo.

Good Place To Land

It is often said, "one thing leads to another." In the case of an early decision to start one development, the rippling effect of its impact has lasted for years.

The history and reasons for the location of CFB North Bay go back to 1933. The Department of National Defence chose North Bay as a regional office for construction of emergency landing fields for a cross-Canada system. This was not an announcement of creating an airport, as there were no national airlines serving Canada at that time. At the outset there was opposition to the airport and Board President, D.J. Morland recommended to council that the cost was too great for the municipality (especially during The Depression). Mr. Morland used the following statements: "too big a venture for the return in sight" and "no guarantee of revenue and a big investment."

What helped change their minds were two things. Senator George Gordon offered to the city a 60-acre plot of land, adjacent to Lee Park and the CPR tracks, for $1200. Also, another location at Emsdale near Burk's Falls was being considered. There was a chance North Bay would be passed by. Obviously others were thinking about the importance of an airport.

The Board quickly responded to the announcement. On April 20, 1933 the Board of Trade passed an important resolution. "That the Board take up with the Department of National Defence position of plans with reference to airport at North Bay area and that we cooperate with municipal council in this matter." It was the beginning of five years of ensuring North Bay be selected as the site as many locations in northeastern Ontario were being considered. It would be a test of the Board's persistence. The federal government policy of that era was not to build airports (passenger terminals) for cities.

Two years later (1935) the position of the Board was strengthened in the resolution, "...request the Hon. E. MacKenzie, Minister of National Defence consider Airport in the vicinity of North Bay and that he be advised that this Board has two sites in view either of which would make an ideal Air Port field. Both have access to one of the main highways which is open the year round, and are within four and a half miles of North Bay." Very shortly thereafter a delegation from the Board journeyed to Ottawa "to investigate the procedure to be undertaken to obtain an Airport for North Bay." In 1936, under the newly formed Department of Transport, the ministry started paving Trans Canada Aerodromes at 100 mile intervals, including the selection of North Bay.

Persuasion paid off. In 1938 the original terminal building was erected giving North Bay the distinction of being the first city in Canada to have a terminal built by the federal government.

A hangar was built in 1939 and the first scheduled flight by Trans Canada Airlines - the forerunner to Air Canada - began April 1, 1940. North Bay was the juncture point for flights from Toronto joining those from Montreal going west. One of the most famous "passengers" was a baby moose being flown from Kapuskasing to the Canadian National Exhibition in Toronto. The stopover in North Bay was a servicing one for the moose and the plane.

The North Bay Airport (1930's) was a big boost to the city and the original building served its purpose until the Jack Garland terminal was constructed. Nipissing Archives/North Bay Area Museum photo.

The outbreak of World War II brought many changes. In 1942 the Royal Air Force Ferry Command took over part of the field as an auxiliary training base. Later an R.C.A.F. ferry detachment was established to fly Liberators and Lancasters across the Atlantic Ocean. The end of the war saw the departure of the R.C.A.F. and civilians became the predominant users of the airport. A new passenger terminal was opened in 1966 and was named the Jack Garland Airport in honour of Hon. J.R. Garland, MP for Nipissing and Minister of National Revenue, who died in 1964.

After the war the Board supported the idea that the airforce have an extended presence in the community. "That owing to the excellent airport facilities here the Department of National Defence be requested to have one of the permanent R.C.A.F. squadrons established in North Bay, and that a copy of this resolution be forwarded to Mr. L. Gauthier, M.P., (January 20, 1946).

The R.C.A.F. returned to North Bay, following the outbreak of hostilities in Korea, when North Bay was chosen to become a regular flying station. The runways and facilities which had been adequate for WWII aricraft were not suitable for the new high performance jet aircraft designed to use the base. Beginning in 1951 the airbase underwent a major face lift. Runways were extended and strengthened, new tarmac, hangars, control tower, living quarters and administrative buildings were constructed.

Above and Below

One of the largest Canadian contributions to the North American Aerospace Defence Command (NORAD) has been the construction and operation of a three-story underground complex, 180 meters (600 feet) deep in the ancient Laurentian mountain range. It plays a vital role in the air defence of North America.

One of the important criteria leading to the choice of North Bay as the site was the close proximity to R.C.A.F. Station North Bay which would supply administrative support and was already in existence.

In 1959 work commenced on the excavation of the huge underground centre of the NORAD system know as Semi-Automatic Ground Environment (SAGE). More than 228,000 cubic meters of Precambrian shield rock were excavated using an unusual Swedish mining technique called, "smooth wall blasting." Construction was completed in 1963 for $51-million.

For years the airport and military operations have been the city's largest employer. The economic impact from the developments of above and underground facilities for more than 60 years has been enormous.

Chamber Manager Glen DeVuono recalls that for years the Chamber and the military community met regularly for social purposes as well as to present each other's point of view. This evolved into the Military Liaison Committee which has retained this aimiable relationship. However, things were not always that way.

During the 1950's there was some resentment in the community towards the base. Fisticuffs were known to have occurred between airmen and the locals over the "stealing of our women."

Base personnel were discouraged form wearing their uniforms off base, however, military haircuts usually gave them away.

In the 1960's the relationship became strained when a Cannex store was established on the base. Base personnel and their families could buy goods considerably cheaper than downtown.

A strong military presence has certainly had a big impact on the community. The CF-100 (without the wing-tip fuel tanks) was a familiar sight in the skies above North Bay. CFB - North Bay has employed hundreds of civilians. The Bomarc missile base on Highway 11 North was one area that was off limits to civilians. This photo - recently released - indicates how the nuclear missile would have been made ready to fire. CFB - North Bay - 22 Wing - Captain Alain Gaudette. Photos on pages 96-99.

A Beginning

It was a big day in the pioneer town.

It may have been one of the most important days in the history of the community. On May 10, 1902, a sod turning ceremony near Trout Lake marked the arrival in North Bay of Temiskaming and Northern Ontario Railway (T&NO). David Purvis, President of the Board of Trade acted as master of ceremonies.

Cover of early North Bay Board of Trade promotional booklet in 1910. Nipissing Archives/North Bay Area Museum photo.

The coming of the Canadian Pacific Railway made North Bay a book title, but the development of the Temiskaming and Northern Ontario Railway gave the writer the material to proceed with the story.

Steam locomotives pulling their cars full of passengers, mail, baggage and freight were an important part of all peoples' lives, whether on the farms, amid the noise and bustle of mining and lumbering communities or in the railway yards of North Bay.

In 1923, two years before North Bay became a city, Mayor John MacDonald, referred to North Bay as a "railroad town." Yet it was not a "company town," where housing and other basic services are owned or directly controlled by the employer. North Bay was during its early beginnings a single enterprise community. For instance, in 1897, of North Bay's 2,024 people, the CPR employed more than 250.

The T&NO or "TNO" as it is referred to by oldtimers, and what would become the ONR (Ontario Northland Railway), has always had a close association with the community. In some "railway families" the government-owned railway has provided the livelihood for three generations of "railroaders."

Early Evolution

For the "boosters" of the North Bay Board of Trade it was known as "Ontario's Development Road," and helped confer upon North Bay its title as "Gateway to the North." Northward through the community moved the people who would establish the towns of New Ontario, southward moved the bounty of minerals and forest products.

From the 1890's onward, provincial government policy greatly influenced the development of the northland. With its vast mineral and forest resources politicians began to realize "New Ontario" as a place for long-term development.

Premier George Ross had to fulfill a campaign promise of opening the northland with a railway. It was soon after the election that the North Bay Board of Trade made sure the government would not forget its promise.

Delegations to Toronto followed for the next two years and the government responded with some preliminary surveys. The $40,000 spent on the evaluation pointed to the development potential in the northland. Faced with another election in 1902, the Liberal government mentioned the railway in a 1901 budget and finally passed the act in 1902. Undoubtedly the province would have been happy for the private sector to construct the much sought after development road. However, the major railroad builders were in the west. Construction of a railway through the rocky Canadian Shield would be a big job with doubtful returns. Faced with the election the government finally announced the construction of the project to be financed by the province.

No sooner was the announcement made, than competition over which way the route would proceed involved the Board of Trade in a second confrontation with Mattawa. The first confrontation was the battle of 1889 between the two communites in their quest to become the district seat, a competition in which even the names of deceased persons were found to be on the voters' lists.

Into this next round of lobbying marched the Board of Trade and other interests in the north on one hand, and ranks of campaigners from Mattawa and Ottawa on the other.

The Mattawa/Ottawa contingent wanted the line to parallel the the old trade route to Lake Temiscaming and have traffic funnelled towards Montreal along the CPR. But there was already a railway line out of Mattawa (Temiskaming Colonization Railroad, early "k" spelling), crossing the Ottawa River and running towards Lake Temiscaming on the Quebec side.

Delegations from North Bay and Toronto quickly pointed out that if Ontario taxpayers were to pay for the railway, it would be in the best interests of all to ensure that Ontario municipalities would benefit. They said it would be a waste of money to have two railways paralleling each other from the same point.

The North Bay contingent promoted the link up with the Grand Trunk Railway which was on a direct line with Toronto. At the same time North Bay had to make sure Nipissing Junction would not become the starting point of the T&NO. Nipissing Junction was already the connecting point of the GTR and CPR. The T&NO would join the GTR but would it run northward on the outskirts of North Bay or through the center of town?

Deputations from council and the Board were heard. North Bay won out. And in a newspaper report several years later the Board of Trade's involvement was highlighted. "This is another enterprise toward which the North Bay Board of Trade bent all its energies, for years, to bring about. Delegation after delegation visited Parliament and gave them no rest"; all for the good of the community.

In Robert Surtees' book, 'The Northern Connection - Ontario Northland since 1902,' he summarizes the economic importance of the terminus location to the town. "The significance of the railway was quite obvious to the people of North Bay, especially to the business community and the town council. It was also patently clear that the greatest advantages would accrue if the new government line were to locate its southern terminal, with its yard, shops, roundhouse, and principal station in the town of North Bay. In terms of payroll income, town development and property, the effect on a small town of only 2,500 persons would be tremendous." The newly formed T&NO Commission also made sure it was known to municipal officials and the Board of Trade that their buildings and facilities would be located on tax-exempt land.

The T&NO had a major impact on North Bay, this 1920 photo shows the round house in the east end railyards. Nipissing Archives/North Bay Area Museum photo.

The "first sod" was turned at the west end of Trout Lake by the Honourable Frank Latchford, Ontario Minister of Public Works. Brass bands lent a festive air to the occasion. With a general election just three weeks away, there was a partisan attitude towards the big event. North Bay's Tory mayor, J.W. Richardson, declined to participate. North Bayites responded by re-electing Liberal John Loughrin.

In a 1967 Nugget article, it says, "Some opinions have also been expressed that the sod turning ceremony was held at Trout Lake because from that point the line could easily be routed to Nipissing Junction should North Bay show a lack of faith on election day."

On July 24 the government announced the formation of a commission to administer the affairs of the railway. A contract was signed with A.R. MacDonnell for construction of the entire line from North Bay to New Liskeard, a distance of 110 miles.

The railway did open the northland as the silver strike in Cobalt showed so well two years later. In 1907 the Board of Trade firmly believed that the proper development of Northern Ontario's mineral resources depended on adequate smelting and refining facilities. The Board was a great "booster" of the Montreal-based firm that constructed a smelter at Trout Mills (Trout Lake), using the adjacent T&NO railway line. By 1909 the smelting operation was producing 50 tons a day of low and middle grade ore using the cyanidization process. The smelter was not profitable and the Board of Trade tried through resolutions to help "overcome the difficulties encountered by private smelters in undertaking to erect smelters in opposition to the great United States companies." But quick returns simply failed to overcome expenses.

The T&NO reached New Liskeard by 1905 and construction was then pushed towards the National Transcontinental line (forerunner to CNR) to Cochrane. Branch lines were constructed to the gold strike in Timmins in 1912, to the Elk Lake silver fields in 1913 and to Iroquois Falls and Abitibi Pulp and Paper Mill in 1913. Clearly the government initiative had served its purpose as a development tool.

On July 15, 1932 the last spike was driven in to mark the completion of the line northward to Moosenee. The dream of a salt-water port on James Bay had been accomplished.

Of significant importance was the change of name from T&NO to Ontario Northland Railway in 1946. This came about mainly because of another T&NO - Texas and New Orleans - cars and accounts were constantly being mixed up. At the same time the Ontario Northland Transportation Commission (ONTC) was established. Included under its jurisdiction: rail services, telecommunications, transport services, express services; and air and marine services - an expanded role in the northland. One such service was the launching of the Chief Commanda in 1946. The all-steel, diesel powered ship had a capacity of 200 passengers and would serve the burgeoning tourist industry of Lake Nipissing and the Upper French River.

It was a day to remember when the original Chief Commanda was launched in Callander, August 20, 1946. It gave a big boost to tourism on Lake Nipissing. Nipissing Archives/North Bay Area Museum photo.

With the help of the Chamber of Commerce, a historical plaque was erected by the province's department of travel and publicity on June 20, 1962. The commemorative plaque erected across from the original limestone headquarters outlined the history and contributions of the ONTC.

The impact of the development of the T&NO and the ONTC remains as an important source of our heritage. North Bay has benefited from this inheritance.

"Nearer" To Near

Today we are included in the travel/tourist area known as the "Near North." It is one way to market a geographic area that has North Bay as its geographic center.

Tourism has always been a major focus of the Board/Chamber and today's concept has roots that date back more than 60 years. With the evolution of the "vacation" and "recreation" North Bay saw itself as a natural destination spot. There were major railway lines to the northland and beyond and it was possible to drive to North Bay from Toronto and further north along the Ferguson Highway. Throughout the 1920's as more Americans journeyed northwards the Board of Trade continued to urge council to establish a permanent information bureau. In January of 1930 a resolution was passed, "that incoming Council advise the City that this Board will contribute $500 towards the maintenance of a Tourist Information Bureau." Council agreed with the Board and an office to serve Northern Ontario was established. At the time it was one-of-a-kind in the North.

A publication produced in 1930 was called: 'The Key to the North,' published by the Board of Trade and printed by the Nugget Press. The booklet was the first large-scale marketing attempt at putting together a strategy to attract tourists to Northern Ontario. The Board saw itself as a leader in this field and promoted the virtues of an area of what we know today as northeastern Ontario.

The Key to the North highlighted tourism in 1939, it was published by the Board of Trade as a supplement to The Nugget. Nipissing Archives/North Bay Area Museum photo.

Camping and fishing in a wilderness theme was the overall message and the writing was very persuasive and in the first person. "I want to get under the green roof of the forest, not over it. I want to catch my trout with fly, not on the fly. I want to hear them sizzling in a frying pan over the glowing coals of a camp fire built where there is just room for it between the granite bluff and the brook-side. I want to argue with the gabby little red squirrels and shoo the rascally whisky jacks away from my bean pot. I want to hear the Loon calling for rain, and the Blue Joint (Jay) whispering to the Mud-hens in the swale. I want to be awakened by the birds at daybreak, roll out of my blanket in time to watch the sun pinning gold lace on the skyline, the green hill-tops peeping through the shimmering mist of morning like timid brides through their veils. I want to climb the hillside at sunset, and look into the west over the top of the forest, when it is rolling green sea with a golden shoreline, when there are great piles of creamy clouds floating in the purple sky above, sprinkled with melted rainbows. I want to sit on a granite craig with my pipe going well and watch it all till it fades and the stars come out."

North Bay received its fair of the promotion. "Let me say to the tourist who seeks rest and quiet among wild and beautiful surroundings, and to the sportsman who would fish and hunt, come to North Bay, get your bearings there. Information will be freely and heartily given you. When you pass through its gates you will have entered an up-to-date city, where you will find accommodation and entertainment to satisfy the most fastidious. At the same time you will have entered the portals of the wide and most splendid natural playground on the continent of North America.

"Ten minutes' drive eastward will bring you to the shore of Trout Lake, Ontario's Lakes of Killarney, the starting point of the famous Mattawa River canoe trip, forty-five miles through woods and waters, teaming with fish and game, splendid in natural scenery.

"Take the steamer Miami Beach at the city dock, sail over beautiful Nipissing and down the wide French into a tourist Eden unsurpassed in the Northland, or elsewhere, far removed from the slightest sound of life's busy whirl.

"Drive up the Ferguson Highway north. In twenty minutes you are passing through a hardwood forest. In half an hour you are among the whispering pines, in a wilderness of lakes, streams, and islands, the beauty no brush could paint.

"Eighteen miles south-east you find the sleepy Nosbonsing, the Red Man's Medicine Lake, where, centuries ago, the tribes of the Nipissing gathered after battle, to bathe their wounds in its healing waters.

"To try to picture what lies about and beyond North Bay to gladden the eye of the tourist, would read too much like far-fetched fiction. We will leave its advertising to the lucky folk who have come, seen, wondered, and enjoyed."

Under the 'Advice' section of the booklet are identified some important points. "Don't pick a guide from the street without previous knowledge of his standing. If he is genuine, he will go with you to the Information Bureau to be approved of by the manager."

And some final advice. "Nature is waiting for you with open arms, arrayed in her best attire. Be careful of your campfires, lest you singe her robes in return for her hospitality.

"Information is not given in this Bureau with a view to holding you at any particular point or resort. The information man will give you the key to the farthest reaches of the North Land if you ask him for it."

The Board of Trade received a "plug." "The members of the Board of Trade are the men who work the pumps keeping the life-current of the city in circulation, an arduous and time consuming duty, self-imposed, not always appreciated by the people who benefit thereby.

"The North Bay Board of Trade have always a good program on their table. With plenty of good material to draw from, the samples in their showcase are well worth looking over. Good business opportunities for men of small capital are plentiful in the Gateway City."

It would be another half-century before tourist operators would see the benefits of marketing the North Bay area as one unit. And in their wisdom they capitalized on past experience and a name that identifies our travel area from the rest of the province. In 1930 the promotional literature explained where travellers would find themselves, "...you will have circled the territory I refer to in this article as the nearer North."

Photos on Page 109:
Top - North Bay got started in the carnival business long ago. At the former CPR park on Oak Street a large ice castle in the background compliments the skating oval under construction. Nipissing Archives/North Bay Area Museum photo.
Bottom - North Bay's first winter carnival was staged by the Northern Ontario Tourist Outfitters in 1946. The downtown core featured a native encampment.

The People's Choice

Merle Dickerson was a man many people will never forget.

He was a man who was enterprising, personable and always controversial by his words and actions. For 37 years since he first sought office he rode the boom and bust cycle of serving the community in a variety of political positions. He was the supreme populist who cared little for convention. He bent the rules and broke the law. He cared for the people and he always believed it was the people who would be the final judge of his actions.

It was his words and actions that set the scene for one of the most unpleasant times experienced by City Council and the Chamber of Commerce.

Relations between the Mayor and the Chamber had been strained for some months in 1954. The Chamber had worked diligently and had been very supportive of the movement to bring a university to North Bay. It appears Mr. Dickerson had been taking a leadership role and it was questionable to the Chamber whether he deserved the credit or not. A pointed and sharply worded resolution was authored by the Chamber: "RESOLVED THAT his Worship Mayor Dickerson be informed that this Chamber of Commerce has been most interested in trying to establish a Universty of Northern Ontario here for a period of five years or more and has been responsible for the completion of an extensive survey on the subject. AND FURTHER, that the Chamber will welcome the assistance of the Mayor in regard to this project and will actively assist in any committee he may wish to form toward the successful conclusion of this project (sic)."

The plot thickened. In October of 1954 the Chamber of Commerce charged that Mayor Dickerson misused his position of authority.

A delegation from the Chamber went before council to request a retraction and apology from the mayor for his comments against the chamber.

The feud stemmed from comments made by Mr. Dickerson, who was a Chamber member. Gerald Alger, Chamber member who lead the delegation said, "this Chamber considers it highly improper that the mayor of North Bay, during a visit to our office, would have suggested that unless treatment inconsistent with present chamber policy should be accorded to his restaurant business, he could use his influences as mayor to interrupt financial arrangements currently existing between city council and the North Bay chamber. (City council each year gave the chamber an operating grant for tourist promotion.) To seek concesssions on such a basis, we say is wrong, and our chamber deplores any such influence or misuse of public office any man elected to administer affairs of this city...If there is any prolongation of this dispute, reponsibility for it certainly cannot be laid at the door of the Chamber of Commerce which now considers the matter closed."

But Mayor Merle Dickerson did not.

In the official minutes of council he said, "This is no place for personalities. The facts are distorted and when I said there were irregularities I wasn't angry. As for the chamber's grant it has been referred to committee and the chamber delegates would be invited to the closed meeting October 26 to discuss the matter further." During the council meeting a resolution was made recommending that the chamber grant be paid. Mayor Dickerson said that the matter was before committee and could not be put forth at council. He finished the debate by stating "he will ask the chamber to show cause why it should receive its grant of $1400 from council." The Chamber did receive its grant and the public issue faded away like so many others in which Mr. Dickerson was involved.

Despite this incident, the 1950's were his "golden years." Mr. Dickerson had arrived in North Bay from Lindsay where he had established an electrical contracting business at the age of nineteen. He was elected to that municipalitiy's electrical commission and was soon charged with doing business with the commission. After a reprimand of two years he was elected to town council, but decided to leave for North Bay in 1938. He arrived in North Bay as a refrigerator salesman and made his first sale to Mayor Jack Shaw. With the outbreak of World War II he joined the army as a second lieutenant and soon made his way to becoming a decorated and distinguished war bond salesman. He found himself in hot water and court martialed when the army discovered that on a furlough he had actively campaigned for former Premier Leslie Frost in his hometown of Lindsay. Newly elected Frost approached Prime Minister Mackenzie King and the charges were dropped.

After being discharged from the army he again returned to North Bay and started his career in real estate, buying, selling and renovating buildings. In 1946 he ran for the North Bay Hydro commission and was defeated. However, in 1947 he was elected as a commissioner and became chairman. In 1948 a Trout Lake sub-station was named after him. During this period he was convicted of tapping hydro lines to bring power to homes he was constructing. An appeal court ruled he had done "nothing illegal."

In 1949, in his first bid for a council seat, he was successful. In 1953 he became mayor and retained that position until 1960. It was during this period he defeated Mayor Nathan Phillips of Toronto for President of the Ontario Mayors and Reeves Association and was named to national executive of the Canadian Federation of Mayors and Municipalities.

Throughout the 1960's and 70's he was in and out of office and twice, unsuccessfully tried to become Nipissing's MPP. It was during this time he was caught in "gaming house" by his own police department. He spent just over two hours in jail and was able to make it to the evening's council session. The eventual conviction only added to his image.

He was removed from office in 1980 after he was found guilty of corrupt election practices during the campaign of 1978. Mr. Dickerson said, "That's the way the cookie crumbles," and vowed that, "I'll be back." He had to wait until 1982 to keep his promise. On the night of his election victory over Dr. Jack Smylie he said he had been "vindicated by the North Bay electorate."

Mayor Merle Dickerson died with his political boots on, June 10, 1984. Only death caused by cancer could remove him from office with no prospect of returning to again represent North Bay.

One of Merle Dickerson's favourite activities was "mainstreeting". This is the Main/Ferguson Street corner (now the Royal Bank). Nipissing Archives/North Bay Area Museum photo.

Mackey House, one of the earliest hotels at the corner of Oak and Ferguson Streets. Nipissing Archives/North Bay Area Museum photo.

Gateway To Opportunity

Consistent commitment to a diverse economic base and strategic location have always been key to the development of North Bay.

It has always been the focus of the Board/Chamber to ensure that the climate of the community has been promoted in a positive manner. For members, it has been in their best interests to attract new ventures to North Bay.

Prior to the 1930's North Bay relied solely on the railways to provide a strong economic base for the community. Industries had not located in Northern Ontario due primarily to proximity to marketplace. New Ontario's vast natural resources were known as the "treasure chest" for the industrial sector of Southern Ontario. Since the turn of the century the economy in Northern Ontario had suffered a "boom and bust" cycle.

North Bay, unlike Sudbury and Sault Ste. Marie, did not have mining resources to attract related industries. It did have a reputation as a transportation centre. North Bay reached a milestone in 1925 when it received its charter as a city. John Ferguson had brought the issue to the Board of Trade as early as March 8, 1914 when he suggested an application be made for a city charter and described the advantages to be derived from city status. As a city with an array of "city services" it had a great ability to borrow money and make decisions on local infrastructure improvements and services. Under the municipal incorporations act the 15,000 population level was relaxed for ambitious communities of "New Ontario" to achieve dignity and independence. This was important to prospective manufacturers.

Early in 1930 the Board of Trade passed a resolution "to appoint a committee to meet the Finance, Water and Light Committee of City Council to place before them the urgency of the appointment of an Industrial Commissioner."

On January 21, 1931 the city announced that a Department of Industry would be established, "devoted to bettering the city in an industrial sense." Former Board of Trade president and North Bay's founder, John Ferguson was appointed as Commissioner of Industries.

In a Nugget article it said, "The duties of the department are to bring the advantages of the city to the attention of manufacturers and other employers of labor with a view to expanding the industrial section." With the formation of such a department, the need for improving water, sewer and power services became more apparent to the municipality.

It is interesting to note the Chamber passed a 1955 resolution, "in favour of the proposed amalgamation," (Widdifield, West Ferris and North Bay) because of the increasing industrial diversification of the area. Amalgamation would become a reality in 1968.

Over the years many industries have located in the Gateway City because of the work of the Board/Chamber and the city. Their histories remain with us today as they remain corporate citizens in the community.

Rahn Metals was initiated by George Rahn and partner H.A. McEwen and was located on the lakeshore in 1929. It became a familiar Northern Ontario manufacturer of bushings, brass, bronze and babitt. Their foundries supplied castings for the pulp and paper and mining sectors. They later expanded into the plastics field producing ducts and pipes that would withstand corrosive processes used in refining operations.

In 1930/31 Canadian Longyear established a manufacturing facility on Regina St. It was a wholly-owned subsidiary of the American company that was formed by E.J. Longyear who performed the first diamond drilling on the Mesabi iron range of Minnesota. In 1947 the company acquired property on Main St. West where the plant produced a wide range of diamond core drills and drilling equipment for world-wide application.

In 1941 the Craig Bit Company (most recently Uniroc, now closed) was formed to manufacture a newly-patented detachable rock-drilling bit to the drill. It was a revolutionary step in the drilling industry. The unique method of connecting the bit to the drill rod was invented by brothers Ernest and Robert Craig, who were raised in Kearney, south of Burk's Falls. In spite of the shortages caused by WWII, the company started at the waterfront. It is a little known fact that during the war the Department of Munitions and Supply asked the plant to produce penetrative caps for six-pound anti-tank shells.

The construction of Nipissing Works (Du Pont, now E.T.I) commenced in 1955 and officially opened July 19, 1957. The plant was located in former Township of West Ferris on a 4,000 acre parcel of land. The plant was equipped to produce an extensive range of explosives to service the mining and construction sectors.

At the time, Johns-Mansville (now Nordfibre) was the only insulating wall board and ceiling tile plant in the province. JM, as it was known in the community, opened in 1957. It relied on the large forest reserves in the Temagami area as a source of wood supply. And with the technology-of-the-day was able to better use poplar and other under-utilized woods for product development. It was the first company in Canada to go into production of non-combustible ceiling panels and tiles.

All industries looked at the excellent transportation facilities provided by the Trans-Canada Highway, the transcontinental lines of both the Canadian Pacific and Canadian National Railways and the north-south line of the Ontario Northland Railway. It was also important that North Bay was centrally located to the rest of Canada, close to major consumer, mining and construction markets.

In 1961 an inaugural meeting of the newly-formed North Bay-Widdifield-West Ferris Department of Industries was held. The establishement of this body was a source of great satisfaction to the District Chamber of Commerce which had been instrumental in convincing the city and the townships of the necessity of such an organization. It was a precursor of what was to evolve. In another seven years the neighbouring townships amalgamated with the city and the North Bay Department of Industries became the forerunner of today's Economic Development Department.

Problem Solver

Terms of political office came and went, and the cars waited, waited and waited. Motorists would call the delays "rest periods."

After a persistent campaign that covered almost two decades, the city finally saw the elimination of its most aggravating traffic problem - the Golf St. crossing.

Replacing the long-time bottleneck is the four-lane overpass that links Main Street with Lakeshore Drive. It was a project on which the Chamber spent a great deal of time and energy until its completion in 1968.

The need to deal with railway traffic was originally addressed in the city's first study compiled by consultants of-the-day in 1928. The formation of a town planning commisssion was a result of pressure applied by the Board of Trade. A sign of a progressive city - suitable to attract industrial and commercial interests - was a municipality with a planned future. In the study it addressed the problem of Golf St. and the connection with the Township of West Ferris. "Further delay in dealing with the situation at the east end of Main Street on the Toronto Highway (now Lakeshore Drive, Highway 11-B) is sure to result in much aggravated inconvenience and possibly otherwise needless loss of life."

For residents travelling to and from the city and West Ferris there would be decades of delays due to the shunting of trains in the CPR and ONR railyards. A preliminary engineering proposal (M.M. Dillon, 1958) said, "The annual cost of maintaining the crossing reportedly in excess of $15,000, and the delay to motor traffic during rush hours has long been a source of irritation to the citizens of North Bay and West Ferris. More recently the steady build-up of traffic volume has aggravated an already bad condition and it is obvious that some remedial measures must be taken in order to maintain the orderly flow of traffic along Main Street and to allow for future development of the urban area."

It was a long time coming and the process would take another ten years. Established in late 1958, members of the joint North Bay-West Ferris Golf Street Overpass Committee started seeking large grants from the federal and provincial governments, and the ONR and CPR to meet preliminary engineering estimates. The Chamber's involvement in the project was acknowledged by the appointment of W.A. Young, he was appointed as a non-voting member of the committee.

The old (pages 118 - 119) and the new (pages 120 - 121). The overpass connecting North Bay and West Ferris solved many traffic problems. Bud Berry - The Nugget collection.

The old (pages 118-119) and the new (pages 120-121). The overpass connecting North Bay and West Ferris solved many traffic problems. Bud Berry - the Nugget.

In the 1950's the Chamber's transportation committee had made the overpass a major focus of its endeavours. There was the problem of who would pay for the overpass, particularly in a post-war period, an era of soaring taxes. The citizens of North Bay and West Ferris had both overwhelmingly voted "for" the bridge in elections. Many municipal elections were fought on the platform of fulfilling the promise of building the overpass, but the tangled web of negotiations continued.

As time marched on, building in the North Bay area and primarily in West Ferris was booming. Most of the homes were occupied by families employed in North Bay, and a consequent increase in the number of cars hurrying to and from the city, made for monumental traffic tieups. Compounding all of this was tourist traffic and the number of trucks carrying loads throughout Northern Ontario. Under the leadership of city council general government committee, headed by Dick Donnelly and city planner Jack Bourne, the maze of commitment was solved. The overpass price tag of $1,634,952.50 was shared between the two municipalities, Transport Canada, the CPR, the ONR and the Department of Highways.

On Friday, October, 18, 1968 Mayor Merle Dickerson and former West Ferris Reeve (now alderman, West Ferris then amalgamated) George Combes cut the ribbon to open the overpass. Whole classrooms of children were there with the hundreds of people there to enjoy the moment. Holding with tradition, a CPR train was seen below holding up the traffic at the Golf St. crossings. Many onlookers admired the view of Lake Nipissing they had never seen before and many knew the wigwags below would soon be forever still.

The Impossible Took Longer

Sometimes progress takes a long time to evolve while the impossible takes a little longer.

This was the case in the formation of the North Bay-Mattawa Conservation Authority, an idea that took a dozen years to materialize, accompanied by a great deal of political will. Note that a conservation authority is a form of regional government.

What started the ball rolling was the flood of 1960. Despite the creation of a wing dam in 1950 at the Chaudiere dam sites (which the Chamber had pressed for) excessive damage occurred, particularly along the West Ferris shoreline. The control of the dams (Department of Public Works) was blamed for the flooding. Fuel was added to the fire of controversy when Reeve George Combes of West Ferris took a flight over the French River and reported the dams were not open.

Concern about the flooding and widespread damage became apparent. The Chamber decided to live up to its "district" affiliation. There was fear that the altered lake level would disturb spawning cycles, a major concern of resort owners. Farmers in West Nipissing were concerned about soil erosion and property owners recognized the loss of docks and property damage.

At a May meeting of 1963, after listening to Mr. A. Barnes, chief of the conservation branch, Department of Lands and Forests, the Chamber made the following suggestion that set the plans in motion to get serious about forming an authority; "That the North Bay and District Chamber of Commerce Special Projects committee look into and possibly guide and promote, if found to be beneficial to all concerned, a Conservation Authority on the east and south side of Lake Nipissing." The main reasons for the Chamber interest included a desire "to preserve and protect our environment for the benefit of local residents and to place this responsibility in the hands of local residents" and "because leisure and vacation time are now increasing and because of our population growth, the demand for such facilities will mushroom. A conservation authority involving parks and recreational sites will be needed to attract tourists." The goals were set, but what was originally envisioned in size and mandate certainly would change during the following nine years of evolution.

A vigorous campaign was launched by the Chamber to establish a conservation authority that included an area of 584 square miles of control. It was too large an area with many municipalities not interested in joining an effort that looked like that it would benefit only North Bay. The initial effort to reach a two-thirds majority amongst municipalities failed. The renewal of effort on a modified scale created a proposal for a South East Conservation

Authority. This attempt, too, developed into an exercise in futility. It was again decided the plan was too big, too unwieldy.

In 1968 a letter was sent by the Chamber's Industrial & Area Development Committee to municipalities which it thought could come together. Part of the letter read: "Various proposals for a conservation area have been made in recent years, but through lack of a common interest among the municipalities little progress has resulted. The proposed conservation area now included the Trout Lake-Mattawa Watersheds and a very small portion of Lake Nipissing."

In 1970 the pot was still simmering. In a June 23, 1970 Nugget article the lead paragraphs alluded to the unsure feeling of establishing an authority. "Most members of North Bay Council are strong supporters of a proposal for establishment of a Conservation Authority. A few are not."

"Ald. Don King called the proposal "another gun pointed to our heads," and Ald. Bill Forth said he would not be in favour unless Ontario Hydro came under the Authority's control, "because Hydro will let the water go, if there are flood conditions, whether there is an Authority or not." Ald. Nel Mallory's concern was with cost, a concern shared by the other two aldermen." But after some debate, council gave its blessing to send two delegates to an organizational meeting.

Delegates had to wait another two years.

It was a joyous occasion on Wednesday, February 16, 1972 when representatives of nine municipalities (North Bay received two votes) voted seven to three in favour of establishing the body. After years of investigation, prodding, planning, meetings and work by Chamber members, the concept became a reality.

Chamber President Ed Vitunski paid tribute in a newsletter, "it should be remembered that one Chamber member in particular, Murray McLean of Northland Engineering, has been the Chamber's most involved member. Past Presidents, too, such as Bill Olmstead, Dick Tafel, Morley Pringle and Murray Leatherdale all have pressed for the formation of the authority."

Surprisingly enough the Chamber of Commerce felt short-changed when the first two representatives of the newly formed North Bay-Mattawa Conservation Authority did not include a Chamber member. President Ed Vitunski in a Sept. 15, 1972 Nugget article said, "If it were not for this Chamber and the efforts of many chamber directors over the years this conservation authority would not be a reality today. This Chamber had to sell the concept of a conservation authority right here in North Bay to the city council. I am disappointed that the efforts of this Chamber were not recognized with the courtesy of allowing this board to recommend several choices from which the general government committee (on city council) could have selected the second delegate."

The Chamber never received its voting privilege and its role continues to fade as the history of the conservation authority continues.

Those magnificent men in their flying machines often landed on Trout Lake in the 1920's. Nipissing Archives/North Bay Area Museum photo.

Voyageur Heritage Saluted

Of all the many special events held during North Bay's Centennial Year, the most exciting to the public seemed to be the three-day Ville-Marie to North Bay Canoe Race.

There was something intriguing about the concept of returning to a past era and making history come alive. It was a colorful way of looking back to this country's early development and recognizing the courage and stamina of the voyageurs who helped with the building of a country.

The Centennial Canoe Race was initiated by the North Bay District Chamber of Commerce and involved chambers in Ville Marie, Temiscaming and Mattawa. Chamber director and former Past-President Richard Tafel co-ordinated the event that attracted professional and amateur paddlers from throughout North America.

The race was described as the toughest canoe challenge on the continent. It included four legs that comprised 120 miles along the Ottawa and Mattawa Rivers. The first leg was Friday, August 18, 47 miles in length from Mission Post Beach in Ville Marie to South Temiscaming (now Temiscaming). The second lap was a 35 mile trip from Thorne to Mattawa down the Ottawa River. On the same day paddlers left Mattawa and raced 11 miles to Samuel de Champlain Provincial Park. The final lap was 27 miles from the park to the Department of Lands and Forests wharf (now Armstrong Beach). Between departure and finsh lines lie some of the most beautiful stretches of wilderness scenery available in the southern part of the province. In the 1970's there was a movement to make Temiscaming-Mattawa part of the Ottawa River a National Park.

It was an ambitious plan that involved a great deal of organization and included battling the elements. It was reported by The Nugget that on the night preceding the race the Ville Marie area was plunged into darkness after a violent storm cut-off electricity. "It meant cold suppers, no refills for cars that had not been adequately supplied with gas when the power broke, no way to dry wet clothing while striking the campground into darkness." For the final briefing the meeting was held by candle light.

Race day saw 27 canoes fighting "six-foot waves on Lake Temiskaming...winds running at 25 miles an hour over the gray, white capped lake took two canoes out of the race in separate dumpings soon after the 27 teams left at 7:45 a.m. Canoes could scarcely be seen by the escort boats because of the high waves. Mr. Tafel said, the canoes were making top speeds of nine miles an hour under conditions that "must be as bad as anything the voyageurs of old ever endured."

The final leg of the race forced the paddlers to face new challenges - portages and the upstream current.

A team of British Columbia paddlers completed the four laps in a combined total of 19 hours, 20 minutes and 30 seconds. They were awarded $850 and $200 in lap prize money.

The initial race was summarized by Mr. Tafel, "It was tremendous success all down the line. We plan to make it an annual," he said. "It was really an inspirational thing. All those in the race really felt they had done something - something that few people have done."

It was an epoch-making event that brought enjoyment to participants and spectators alike. It was a way of promoting the area and the heritage of the aboriginals, explorers and voyageurs who utilized the Nipissing passageway. In time, the three-day marathon was marked by special festivities along its route, that created a "carnival" atmosphere in the four participating communities. Although the organizers viewed the race as a major event, it became harder to find a sponsor that would provide the money to attract top professional canoeists.

What remains today is a long lasting racing heritage, the North Bay-Mattawa Canoe Race sponsored by the North Bay-Mattawa Conservation Authority. It is run every August and remains as one of the oldest marathon canoe races in North America.

Resource Protection

The yearly cycle of angling continues on Lake Nipissing, almost a four-season recreational pursuit.

The yellow pickerel (walleye) have been sought for hundreds of years, first by aboriginals, the Nipissings, who made their summer home the north shore of Lake Nipissing. To the early Jesuits the fish were called "dore" or "dory," meaning gilt or golden.

In 1933 the Board of Trade aggressively started their promotional efforts. A report entitled, 'More and Better Tourist Trade,' states, "More aggressiveness in establishing the importance and appeal of Lake Nipissing and adjoining fishing waters, along with bathing houses and seating facilites at the Amelia Park Beach." Other recommendations included the provision of more road signs for greater visibility along the newly constructed Trans Canada Highway, and a fish hatchery to help re-stock area lakes.

With the birth of the Dionne Quintuplets in 1934, our local tourist industry was launched. Thousands of Canadians and Americans spent their two-week vacations bathing in the warm waters and lying on the lake's sandy beaches. Former Chamber secretary/manager, Mel Mellow (1958-66) calls Nipissing, "North Bay's luckiest boost!" It was also the start of an international reputation for the lake - known as one of the best sources of the savoury pickerel flesh, one of the most important sport fish in North America. Tourist lodges, cabins and motels dotted the shoreline.

In 1950 the Chamber of Commerce made a resolution that partially foretold the changing state of the Lake Nipissing fishery. "That due to the ever-increasing pressure on the game fish supply of Lake Nipissing, by angling, leaving the coarse fish, ling, eel, gar pike, sheeps head and suckers, to increase to such an alarming extent, that we ask the Department of Lands and Forests to commence a project for the removal of these coarse fish, in order to balance the fish population, giving the game fish a better chance of survival, both from natural propagation and restocking." It was a long sentence, but it wouldn't take long for many people to see that the lake's fishery might be in jeopardy.

By the late 1960's the rumblings had started. It was becoming apparent the fish population was diminishing in size and number. With approximately 80% of the total amount of tourist dollars spent in the area directly attributed to Lake Nipissing it was clear something had to be done. It became apparent the fishery was headed for trouble unless intensive management of the resource was started immediately.

A 1972 report by the tourist committee of the Chamber considered the need to reduce the length of the fishing season, particularly in the winter. Also, there was concern of the ratio of coarse fish to pickerel estimated at four to every one pickerel.

In response, Ministry of Natural Resources biologist, Roger Wolfe, addressed the concerns at meeting of directors of the Chamber. He said, "Lake Nipissing is not being fished out, we are not concerned to the point that we feel a tragedy is about to occur." He also said, "Winter fishing is not the major factor."

Recommended by the Chamber was a 21-member Lake Nipissing Resources Council. In February of 1973, director John Lyle said, "Some kind of management structure is needed at the local level, there is none at the moment." The aim of the council was to represent all interests on the lake and provide the ministry with input regarding improvements to the lake, in areas of local concern. In February of 1973, Parry Sound MPP Lorne Maeck, North Bay District Forester Don Vance, Chamber President Bryan Manson and Nipissing MPP Dick Smith met with Leo Bernier, Minister of Natural Resources. The Lake Nipissing Advisory Committee became a reality.

John Lyle, President of the Chamber in 1974, headed the advisory committtee. Biologist, Carsten Jorgensen's report indicated "serious overharvesting of Lake Nipissing's pickerel population." Working cooperatively with the ministry, recommendations were made and implemented, the fishing season was shortened, sanctuaries were expanded and protected. The results have paid dividends; the working group established has helped manage one of the province's most important, four-season fisheries.

Big Dig

It was called the "big dig" and it transformed and preserved the downtown core of the city as a vibrant and important part of the community.

The Masons parade proceeded even though the Main Street was experiencing a "dig" circa 1905. Nipissing Archives/North Bay Area Museum photo.

In the 1960's and 70's, plaza, mall and strip development had begun to evolve on the North Bay landscape. Shopping trends started to change away from the traditional downtown core of the city. The center of the community had changed little during previous decades. At the same time city council was dealing with upgrading sewer, water and underground hydro infrastructure that had been around since the early 1900's. In fact, the last major facelift occurred in 1920-21 when Main St. was paved and sidewalks were constructed. There was so much civic pride that during a summer festival motor cars were prohibited from driving on the newly surfaced areas for fear of leaking oil and gasoline and thereby damaging the new pavement.

In 1906 the Board of Trade successfully petitioned city council to recognize the downtown core in two ways, one being light standards and the second being the official declaration of a business section: "as those blocks between Sherbrooke and Foran Sts., on Main St., from Ferguson to Fraser St., from Oak to McIntyre St., on Klock (Algonquin Ave.) and from Oak St. to McIntyre on Fraser St."

The "sport shirt parade" was a popular event in 1957, a good way to promote the downtown and the summer tourist season. Peter and Pam Handley collection.

In 1978 the Chamber would support members situated in the downtown area who were faced with a municipal servicing program that would disrupt Main St. during four consecutive summers. Leaders of the Progressive Business Guild (formed in 1975), which represented the central shopping district, declared their intentions to change the scheduled Main St. public works program. It was formed at the urging of the Chamber.

Paul Lafrance, chairman of the Business Guild warned, "It's the most major issue we'll be faced with in our lifetimes in the downtown core. At the end of it, we're going to see a lot of new faces (downtown store owners) because a lot of the old ones aren't going to make it. If people break their shopping habits, we've lost them for good." The downtown core represented about 25 per cent of North Bay's total tax base.

Mr. Lafrance said it was the task of the guild representatives to make council aware of the importance of the downtown area and aware of the opinions of the business owners operating there.

They did.

The entire process included public meetings almost a year before the first shovel went to work. Input from residents, shoppers and businesses was solicited for their view of what a highly, visible downtown area should include.

What evolved was a newly-formed Downtown Improvement Area (DIA); merchants worked with city council for a concept that called for wider sidewalks, paving stones, mid-block crossways, new lighting, benches, kiosks and a variety of trees and bushes, giving a more pleasant appearance to the downtown area. The DIA would also initiate a separate tax for the downtown area which would help in the redevelopment process. And instead of four years, seven months were needed to complete the majority of disruptive construction. Original estimate of the project was $3.2-million, but a $500,000 overrun was incurred.

On May 10 of 1983 DIA Chairman, Gary Lennox helped smash a bottle of champagne against a giant scoop to officially launch Main St. reconstruction. On hand were MPP Mike Harris, Alderman Jim Kelly, deputy city engineer Brian Baker and Chamber President, Hugh McLachan. Six months later they staged another celebration to mark the end of the first phase of the project.

On October 30, 1984, North Bay Hydro poles and overhead wires were removed, the last vestiges of a past era were gone and a new beginning was complete.

Photos on Page 133:
Top: Many people will remember the decorative foyer of the Capitol Theatre, now the city's Arts Centre. Known as the "palace of splendour" it opened in 1929, as the third largest theatre in Ontario featuring North Bay's first "talkie" 'In Old Arizona'. Nipissing Archives/North Bay Area Museum photo.
Bottom: One of the innovative ways to get the community in the Christmas spirit was an extensive Christmas lighting campaign. In the photo are: Bruce McLeod, Bruce Goulet, Keith Packer, Graham Parker, Bill Morland and Al Jackson.

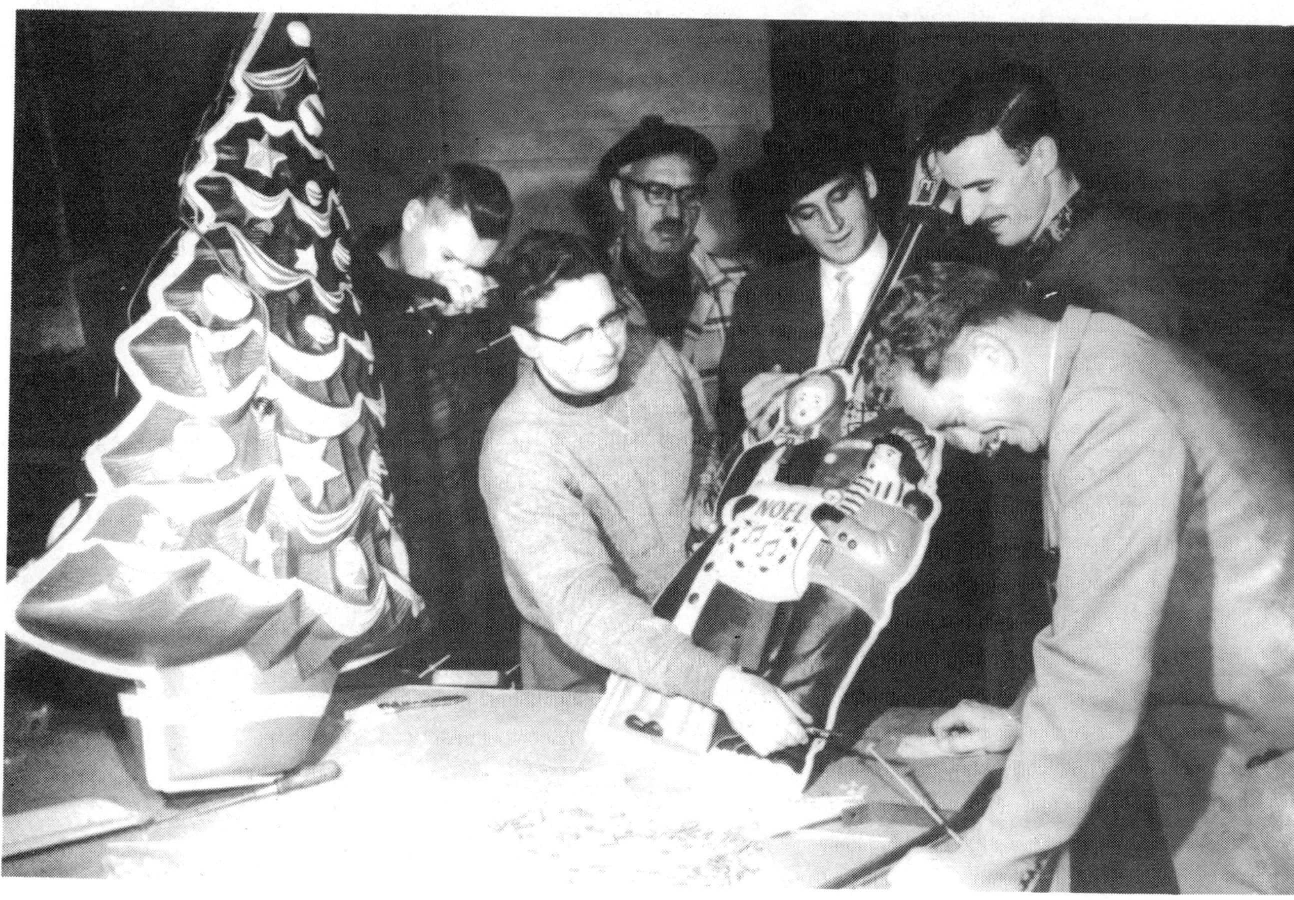
NOEL

ROYA

The Boer War, started in 1899, was not forgotten in North Bay. These "Save Our Empire" supporters are seen outside the Royal Theatre (Sibbitt building) on Main Street, circa the turn of the century. Nipissing Archives/North Bay Area Museum photo.

It Takes Time

Nipissing University's charter effort was a long time in the making. There were people, power and politics in the way of self-determination.

In 1946 the Board of Trade had played a significant role in rallying public support and interest in the idea of having an automonous university in the community. In 1947, a committee was formed under the leadership of Walter Little (later to become a District of Parry Sound judge), representing the Board of Trade, set out to assess the validity of having such an institution. An unpublished document, 'A University Is Born' compiled by the late Father Ted Sobisch and the book, 'Nipissing University College - Through The Years', by Ina Hutchison document the trials and tribulations leading to the affiliation of what was once Northeastern University with Laurentian University in Sudbury. It was the beginning of Nipissing University College and finally the charter making it Canada's newest university.

Early Beginnings

A far-sighted group of local citizens formed a committee in 1946 to seek university education in North Bay. But two other earlier developments helped lead to the eventual pursuit of an institution for higher education.

It helped bring higher education to North Bay. The North Bay Normal School (now Correctional Services) has always been a North Bay landmark. Nipissing Archives/North Bay Area Museum photo.

It really began in 1909 when the North Bay Normal and Model School was opened, in what is today the home for the Ministry of Correctional Services. The Board of Trade had been big supporters of the school and pressed for its location in North Bay. As the silver boom in Cobalt and the Temiskaming and Northern Ontario Railway opened "New Ontario" people poured into the north. Teachers were scarce.

The province's department of education offered all those who enrolled $1 per day in expenses. Hundreds of young women and men took advantage of this liberal assistance while attaining their teacher training. The eventual joining of the teachers' college in 1972 with Nipissing University College produced a faculty of education with a long standing reputation for offering a quality program.

The second development includes the forward thinking of one man the community owes a great deal. Reverend Norman J. Weaver, President of North Bay College (Scollard Hall). He, as Father Sobisch states, "was destined through his vision, his knowledge, his wisdom and his courage to become the leader that would bring university education to North Bay." (The Norman Weaver Auditorium at the university is dedicated to the memory of Father Weaver.)

Father Weaver had long realized that the young people in the North did not have the same opportunity to obtain a university education as those in southern Ontario. Scollard Hall was opened in September of 1931 and incorporated in 1934. As Father Weaver explained, the charter granted the local institution the opportunity to carry on work at the university level.

From 1949 until the late 1950's the University of Toronto established a "junior varsity" at North Bay College. It was the initiation of university education and the issuing of Pass Degrees in Arts through the University of Toronto.

Politics Prevail

In March of 1958 the North Bay and District Chamber of Commerce established a committee to create public interest in establishing a local university. The Northeastern University committee was formed. By 1960, 15 first-year university subjects were offered to 27 day and 85 evening students. It was then thought royal assent would be granted to Northeastern University as a non-denominational, degree-granting institution.

Throughout the history of development of Northern Ontario there has always been an air of competition between North Bay and Sudbury. It was evident in the battle for higher education in the late 1950's.

Arrangements had been made to secure approximately 500 acres of Crown land north of the city for the future university, (negotiations with the Nipissing Indian Band failed to locate the proposed university on the lakeshore.) But the ambitious plans for a bilingual university in Sudbury were coming to light.

To ensure progress and support from various religious denominations, the United Church, the Anglican Church and the Society of Jesus were invited to establish colleges on the same campus and federate with the university concept called "Laurentian."

As Father Sobisch states, "rumours were spreading rapidly throughout the north country regarding the monopoly Sudbury was going to have on university education."

Support for a new facility, Huntington College, was proposed for the University of Sudbury, it also included Sacred Heart College, operated by the Jesuit Fathers of the French Province of Eastern Canada, affiliated with Laval University in Quebec City. Although this order was the dominant force in developing a bilingual university, the province would not fund one, church-related university. Additional interest and strong lobbying forces were brought forth by the United and Anglican Churches.

Additional support was steadily increasing from senior executives of large companies such as INCO and Falconbridge. Large financial commitments paved the way for new facilities. At the same time government officials had to consider locating Huntington College in North Bay. It would have been federated with North Bay College, operated by the English Fathers of the Resurrection whose headquarters were in Waterloo (St. Jerome's College).

When representatives from Northeastern University and North Bay College appeared before the Private Bills Committee of the Ontario Legislature they were informed of the "special opposition" from the Sudbury presbytery. Father Sobisch notes: "It was understood that opposition had been registered through various channels by certain influences within Laurentian University." The application by the North Bay contingent was turned down.

Laurentian gained university status through a federation of church-sponsored colleges in 1960. Northeastern University continued to offer "night courses" for year one and two programs form 1962 to 1967 at the vacated North Bay Home for the Aged known as "Cassellholme" location. However, the need for students to complete degrees started in North Bay was becoming apparent.

In 1966 President Stanley Mullins of Laurentian University outlined what affiliation would mean to Northeastern University. "Academically, Northeastern would be totally dependent on Laurentian for direction and policy. Financially, Northeastern would be semi-dependent submitting its own budgets, but making its own requests through Laurentian. Administratively, Northeastern would be free." This remained as the basic operating arrangements through the

1980's.

Dream Comes Of Age

In 1967, Northeastern University became affiliated with Laurentian. Forty-nine full-time students began their studies at the refurbished Casselholme location.

The dream of the 1947 committee was starting to come true.

In Ina Hutchison's book, she states, "In November (1967) during a visit to North Bay, William Davis, who was introduced by H.E. Brown (long time chamber member and board representative), discussed plans with the North Bay District Chamber of Commerce for extending the educational system by establishing a post secondary complex at North Bay." Mr. Brown would later serve as the Chairman of the Board of Governors from 1975-1984.

It would be another five years until the College Education Centre was completed on top of the escarpment. Another important person in the evolution of university education, Jack Trussler, chairman of the then board of governors likened the lengthy struggle to the "Battle of Waterloo." His vision of a new facility including the teachers' college, St. Joseph School of Nursing, Cambrian College (Canadore) and the university college came true in 1972.

Also, the name changed. In place of Northeastern, such names as Algonquin, Champlain, Chippewa, Northland and even Gateway were suggested. The name, "Nipissing" was selected as being the most appropriate because of the historical association of the Nipissing Indians and the geographical location of the Nipissing passageway.

In 1990, 1517 students, including 1000 full-time students took advantage of more than 200 courses offered on and off campus. Statistics proved it was the fastest growing post-secondary institution in the province.

Leading up to 1992 there were many meetings with government officials visiting North Bay. They learned Nipissing College had served its apprenticeship well with Laurentian. The senate and board of governors of Nipissing knew it was ready to grant its own degrees. It became an independent university on December 10, 1992.

Almost a half-century of determination by the founders has prevailed, Nipissing has come of age and remains the 'Path to Knowledge'.

Community Additions

Throughout our history there have been many projects to which the Board of Trade/Chamber of Commerce have lent their support. The efforts usually meant "boosting" the idea throughout the community and contributing the hard work of members to make a good idea go forward. We can't forget the efforts of the past because their endeavours remain with us.

"Chippewa Barracks"

Many citizens will remember social events and weddings at the Chippewa Barracks and its earliest beginnings start well before World War II.

It is not apparent why the Board of Trade authored the following resolution on August 21, 1931. "Resolution passed that a recommendation be forwarded to the Federal Government that a suitable Armory at North Bay be constructed and that a militia unit be established here."

World War II was far from being a reality and the "Great War" was becoming a memory. The Algonquin Regiment had served in 1916/17. Two battalions were recruited and the town covered each man with a life insurance policy for $1,000. Memorial Park was established in 1927 and Remembrance Day was adopted in 1931. There was no major army base in Northern Ontario and perhaps our forefathers saw an opportunity to better the community with such a facility? Certainly, as the war approached, the new North Bay airport (1938) would be considered when making such a decision. The Board of Trade had long lobbied to have an airport in the community. Air transport of troops and munitions was becoming a reality.

On August 14, 1940 North Bay was selected as a training centre for men called for compulsory military duty. Overnight, the Rosedale Park location was turned into a field of activity with more than 300 carpenters constructing huts, kitchens, a recreation centre and camp hospital. Speed was of the essence. The site - Fort Chippewa Barracks - (Canadian Army Training Centre #22) was ready to receive recruits by October. It was a busy place during the war and the community made a great effort to make army personnel feel at home.

As the war drew to a close the Board of Trade passed a resolution, October 18, 1945, with an eye to the future. "That a resolution be sent to the Minister of National Defence at Ottawa asking that consideration be given to stationing at North Bay a regiment of troops, such as might be deemed necessary under current plans for a permanent army force to be maintained

Off they went to the Great War. These soldiers were marching along Main Street, just outside the Continental Hotel. Nipissing Archives/North Bay Area Museum photo.

in Canada, and that if this suggestion meets with the approval of the Minister that the regiment stationed here be named 'The Algonquins' in order to perpetuate the name of the regiment which went overseas during the Second World War 1939-45 from Northern Ontario. We would also point out there is now excellent accomodation for a regiment in North Bay since an army camp was erected here during the war, and is still available for use. An even larger number of men could be stationed here since the accomodation is available, and since North Bay, the Gateway to the North, is ideally situated to serve all of Northern Ontario." At war's end the Algonquins counted 341 dead and 959 wounded or missing: this high toll from just over 4,000 men who served with the battalion from its mobilization on July 22, 1940 to its return to North Bay on January 29, 1946.

The wish was partially fulfilled as the regimental headquarters of "A" Company of the Algonquin Regiment would find a home there. It was again suggested by the Chamber of Commerce in 1952 through M.P. Jack Garland that the government consider establishing an armory. But it would be a while coming. Over the years the valuable property would be developed and be taken over by Chippewa Secondary School, Cite des Jeunes, Ontario Provincial Police district headquarters and the Barclay House, a retirement home. The original intent of the area has certainly changed in a half-century of development.

These soldiers were enjoying a little time with friends at the government dock in 1916. Nipissing Archives/North Bay Area Museum photo.

The official opening of the $2.7 million, Major Leo Troy Armory was held in June of 1983, a distant link with the original Fort Chippewa. It was the same Captain Leo Troy of the Algonquin Regiment who received $500 from city council in 1940 for "recreational purposes," and would represent the Nipissing riding as our M.P.P. in 1959.

Showplace Of The North

Our community arena is the envy of many cities in the northland; its appearance reflects the care given to it for almost forty years.

It was a costly project - almost $800,000 - and the decision to construct Memorial Gardens had to be put on a municipal ballot. In April of 1953 the Chamber had supported the city's Athletic Parks Commission's report (APC) on the building of the costly venture.

The vote in 1954 was For 1,872; Against 1,519.

Once adopted by the citizens at the polls, hockey, figure skating and other events moved to the brand new headquarters. Previous to this the "King Street" arena had seen service for

Like most communities in Northern Ontario, North Bay was proud of its 1923-24 Junior NOHA Champions. Nipissing Archives/ North Bay Area Museum photo.

almost 20 years and before that there was an arena on Main St. West built in 1905.

In 1933 the Board of Trade supported the following proposal, "This Board hopes that the time will not be far distant when some definite form of securing a hockey and skating arena in North Bay will be presented." It was in the same year that a group of Board of Trade members headed by former Board President and Mayor, J.H. McDonald formed a group - called the Promoters of North Bay Rink and Auditorium Co. Ltd. - looking for the opportunity to approach the North Bay electorate with the idea of a fixed assessment of taxes to develop a facility through private means. Although "The Depression" was on, council somehow found enough money to construct the new arena in 1936.

It was not until 1951 that a community recreational council (APC) was appointed by city council, including Chamber President, A. Lafrance, to investigate the possibilities of a community centre with artificial ice.

In four years the new arena would become a reality. The Honorable Vincent Massey, Governor General of Canada dropped the puck when the Senior North Bay Trappers met the Sudbury Wolves, October 29, 1955. Ab Demarco was the North Bay center for the opening ceremony. The official party included: Phillip Kelly, minister of mines for the province, North Bay Mayor, Merle Dickerson, Conn Smythe, representing the National Hockey League, architect Howard O'Gorman, Harry Smith, chairman of the city's parks and recreation committee, Clarence Rennick, building committee chairman and the Garden's manager, Howard Radford.

It was Howard Radford who established the work ethic of thorough maintenance that kept Memorial Gardens "like new." This tradition was carried on by former managers Morris Synder and Terry Talentino. It is because of its "spotless" appearance that it has attracted a number of prestigeous events such as the Canadian Figure Skating Championships in 1964 and 1986.

The list of entertainers that have performed bring back memories: Nana Mouskouri, Carroll Baker, Charlie Pride, Roger Whittaker, April Wine, Murray McLaughlin, Anne Murray, Stompin Tom Connors, Jackie Vernon, Irish Rovers, George Hamilton, Neil Diamond, Ernest Tubb, Roy Acuff, Liberace, Victor Borge, Gordon Lightfoot, Shrine Circus, Garden Bros. Circus, Pig and Whistle Show, Canadian Forces and NORAD bands, Ice Capades, Stars On Ice, Ray Price, Kitty Wells, Louis Armstrong, Hank Snow, Guy Lombardo, Jerry Lee Lewis, Marty Robbins, Bill Haley and the Comets, Bobby Curtola, Don Messer and Kenny Rogers.

Memorial Gardens has been home to the North Bay Trappers of junior, senior and professional (1961-62) hockey leagues, and has been home to the North Bay Centennials since 1982. The North Bay Figure Skating Club has been part of both arenas since 1941.

"O.H."

It was an example where the newly named "Chamber of Commerce" (1948) wasted no time in organizing support for an idea that would bring an important facility to Northeastern Ontario.

A December 8, 1949 resolution read: "That this Chamber of Commerce make strong representations to get the Minister of Health to have located in or near North Bay the new mental hospital proposed for Northern Ontario. And further, that a special committee be set up to secure this hospital. And, that copies of this resolution be sent to the Hon. Russell T. Kelley, Minister of Health for Ontario; W. Harvey, M.P.P. for Nipissing; and to His Worship the Mayor and members of City Council."

It would take a few years of lobbying before the site and decision was made in favour of the Highway 11-North location. And it would not be until October 15, 1957 that the Ontario Hospital opened making it the largest provincial public service employer in the area. Located on 164 acres the site was comprised of the administrative building and four pavilions and a nurses residence.

The 1,200 bed-Ontario Hospital (locally known as the "O.H.") was declared officially open by Nipissing M.P., John Chaput as he cut the ribbon in front of 1,500 persons. At the time it was widely believed to be the finest facility of its kind in North America. It employed 400 persons.

The Lord's Nostalgic Day

The people of North Bay received a Dominion Day birthday present in the Centennial Year of 1967 from Lord Thomson of Fleet. Approximately one-half the cost of the new YMCA pool and a $10,000 donation for needy children using the facility was given to the community.

Roy Thomson was a former Board of Trade member, alderman and mayorality candidate in 1933. His platform was one of tighter finance, but the conservative railway community continued its tradition of returning a successful mayor for a second term. His radio station CFCH started in 1931 situated in the Capital Theatre. It was the pioneer station of Northern Ontario with a 50-watt transmitter. The Board of Trade quickly supported its member with a resolution, "passed that this Board heartily endorse the application of CFCH for license to increase its wave length form 50 to 500 watts and that a copy of the resolution be forwarded to Hon. Mr. Duranleau, Minister of Marine."

It was also the bleakest of times for the City of North Bay. North Bay had expended too much money to help those needing relief and by 1935 it had taken its toll. The province's municipal board took over the management of municipal finances. The matter of "relief" was one Roy Thomson did not entirely believe in - although as an alderman he headed the city's relief committee for two years. He was known to have said, "I don't believe in relief...and they should suffer a little." The Board of Trade indignantly supported City Council. "At the request of President Thomas M. Mulligan, Mayor Bullbrook addressed the meeting and very carefully explained the recent order of the Ontario Government which placed North Bay under the supervision of the Ontario Municipal Board. Several members took part in this discussion and the Board indicated their willingness to assist the North Bay council in an endeavour to have the order removed as it has been clearly shown that the City of North Bay never at any time defaulted interest or principal payments on outstanding debentures." It was shortly thereafter Roy Thomson resigned from council and moved away to bigger things.

His meteoric rise in the media world was greatly influenced by his time in the North Bay area. In 1967 he remembered "pounding the pavement looking for buyers of radio spots." He paid tribute to the Board/Chamber's longest serving member (52 years in 1974), Sol Waiser, "as one of my earliest supporters."

In 1960 Roy Thomson bought CKGN-Channel 10, it had gone on the air December 19. 1956.

On July 1, 1967, after a 30-year absence from Northern Ontario, he returned, and helped make the community 'Y' a reality.

Another Catch

It was developed in 1937 and although it is now known as a "fish culture station" it has always been known to us as the "fish hatchery" just out of Balsam Creek.

In addition to visiting Quintland (late 1930's and early 1940's), the fish hatchery was considered as one of the area's other attractions; thousands of tourists have travelled Highway 63 to see for themselves how trout are raised and how fish stocking helps contribute to the tourist economy of northeastern Ontario.

Again the Board of Trade wasted no time in helping one of their most important causes of all time - tourism. In February, 1930, they resolved "that the Fisheries and Tourist Committee be authorized to appoint a delegate to meet Deputy Minister of Game and Fisheries at Toronto to urge the necessity of establishing a hatchery at North Bay."

The idea became a reality as the Department of Lands and Forests opened the North Bay

The fish hatchery has entertained thousands of tourists since it opened in 1937. In 1950 ice was taken from Twenty Minute Lake to keep water cool during shipments. Gary Preston - MNR photo.

Trout Rearing Station in 1937.

It may have been a coincidence or very timely, but in September of the same year the province opened the North Bay-Temiscaming highway (Highway #63). It was another project the Board of Trade had initiated and worked diligently on for almost a decade. It was one reason why the hatchery was located outside of Balsam Creek, along with the abundance of natural springs.

Feeding The Elk

With the government hatchery in place the Board of Trade came up with the idea of importing a herd of elk from a federal farm near Petawawa, with a view to stocking the district with a new species. The original herd included three cows and two bulls.

In a 1939 'Old Home Week' program it described the state of the herd. "For the tourist who is interested in wild life and likes to do his shooting with a camera, a trip to the government fish hatchery of the North Bay-Timiscaming highway, 23 miles from the city, would prove highly interesting, for there, in the protection of the hatchery grounds, a herd of fine elk has been released. The presence of salt licks and fodder at the hatchery have proved such an attraction to the creatures that they can often be seen in the immediate vicinity of the hatchery, although they are free to roam through miles of wild bush land. The Ontario government has declared an indefinite closed season of hunting the animals and they are breeding and spreading in the region unmolested. Under protection it is believed they will soon be as plentiful as deer."

In an extremely cold winter an article appeared in the Nugget with the headline, 'Board of Trade Provides Fodder for Imported Animals.' "The small herd of elk 'pets' of the North Bay Board of Trade will not go short of food this winter. Because winter conditions have made it increasingly difficult to forage for food in their home territory near the Balsam Creek fish hatchery, a load of hay has been stacked where the animals can eat it. The Christmas box was sent to the hatchery by the Board."

The size of the herd grew and the elk began to wander away from their original home. In the 1950's a parasite, "liver fluke" was discovered in cattle in the North Bay area. It was believed that cattle were contracting the parasite from the elk which were known to graze in the farm fields. A controlled hunt was organized and the herd was eliminated during the following years.

The opening of North Bay's first Legion entertained the Governor General His Grace the Duke of Devonshire in 1920. John Ferguson is the second person sitting from the left. Nipissing Archives/North Bay Area Museum photo.

This time
WE ARE ALL IN
FRONT LINE
Give us the tools
AND WE WILL
FINISH THE JOB
OF NOVA SCOTIA
OCHRANE DUNLOP HARDWARE
LIMITED

Photo on Page 150 and Above: Outside and inside the Cochrane Dunlop building during World War II promoting one of the war time conferences between President Roosevelt, King George VI and Prime Minister Winston Churchill. Nipissing Archives/North Bay Area Museum photos.

Organized sport has always been important in the community. This is a team photo of the 1927 Canadian Pacific Railway softball club. Nipissing Archives/North Bay Area Museum photo.

They made North Bay proud. The Rinkey Dinks became the Northern Ontario Softball champions of the province in 1929. Nipissing Archives/North Bay Area Museum photo.

Three Men And The Buildings

Some things and some people stay with us for a long time. Memories are created by their presence.

In 1944 the Board of Trade entered their first home and began the second half of a century "boosting" and serving the community.

Prior to 1944 all of the secretarial and office administration was accomplished by part-time workers and the directors. Directors Les Banner and Harry Desjardins were two hard-working individuals who took on much of the office administration in earlier times. The Board decided to hire the first of three employees who would provide leadership for the next half-century.

Bruce

Bruce McLeod will be long remembered for his cigars and much more.

He was hired in 1944 on a part-time basis as the Board's public relations/secretary officer, an arrangement that continued throughout his years with the Board/Chamber. At the same time he continued his writing career which had seen him work for The Nugget, Roy Thomson's CFCH and as an assistant editor for McLean's Magazine.

"Initially my part-time retainer was $60.00 per month. The log cabin information bureau was heated only by a coal-burning stove. It had to be stoked nightly and the ashes removed daily during the winter months. A new oil burner was cause to celebrate by the staff."

Over the years board of directors meetings were held monthly at several different locations including the Board Room of the St. Regis Hotel; the Cloud Room at the Empire Hotel and a meeting room at the Belmont Hotel. Annual meetings at the Empire featured a variety of dignitaries - ranging from Lester Pearson and Paul Martin to Donald Keyhone the "Flying Saucer" expert. "Perhaps the most boring speaker to address one of our annual meetings was an economist from one of Canada's chartered banks. As one of the Directors remarked after the ordeal, 'Well, you can't win 'em all.'"

Bruce would continue in North Bay as station manager for CKGN-TV. He later returned to North Bay to develop CKAT in 1967 and eventually acted as executive director of North Bay's Downtown Improvement Area.

One of the feathers in his cap was the organization and promotion of the largest conventions ever to be staged in North Bay - the North America Outdoor Writers. Working with

Secretary-Manager, Bruce McLeod, was presented with a gold watch by President Al Jackson when he left the Chamber in 1958 to Manage CKGN-TV.

the Northern Ontario Tourist Outfitters (NOTO), the Chamber attracted outdoor columnists from Canada, United States and Mexico. "The 1949 event was worth several million dollars of direct and indirect publicity for the North Bay area." Long serving Director, Hartley Trussler chaired the organizing committee.

Another endeavour started an eventual tradition. In 1946, a winter carnival was organized through the Northern Ontario Tourist Outfitters because they were staging a conference in North Bay. It was followed in 1947 with an event, privately financed by Bruce and Peter Orfankos, working in co-operation with the Kinsmen Club and the Board of Trade. It would not be until 1965 that the Chamber would help initiate the North Bay Winter Fur Carnival and the "Duke the Toque" character and logo.

One of the highlights of the 1947 carnival was the "Whiskerinos" - King of the Whopping Whiskers. It was a beard growing contest that received national attention in the media especially with the issue of "no whisker permits." Bearburgers were a popular item at the carnival under the slogan, "try bruin-on-the-bun." So were the North Ski Championships at Laurentian Ski Club featuring two ski jumps.

During the years between 1945 to 1957 the Board/Chamber was responsible for all of the city's tourist promotion, and much of the drive for new industrial growth. Bruce originated the phrase: "On the Crossroads to Everywhere," in recognition of the fact that North Bay was a busy rail hub; on Highway 11 and the Trans Canada Highway, while having a large airport. "We pretty much financed all the promotional efforts as our annual grant from the city was about $3,000."

"We did a 'selling job' for the North Bay District at various Sport Shows - in Cleveland, Buffalo, Chicago and Toronto. Chamber members and directors volunteered their time to staff the exhibits. We serviced thousands of business and tourist inquiries every year; made reservations for vacation visitors at lodges, motels, hotels, cabins and fish-hunt camps."

Before the push of energy conservation, the Chamber undertook street lighting and decoration campaigns designed to establish North Bay as "Ontario's Christmas City."

"Under the leadership of President Keith Packer, Chamber volunteers cut and trucked several hundred small evergreens into the city from adjacent highway right-of-ways where the Department of Highways had decided to remove them as scrub growth. These little trees were then attached to parking meters along Main and other streets in the downtown business area, making a 'Christmassy decor.' Several thousand dollars were spent on illuminated street decorations, plastic candles, snowmen, Santas, reindeer, angels and carollers. With the cooperation of the North Bay Hydro Commission these were mounted on hydro poles. An official 'lights on' ceremony was held and serveral thousand people would turn out for the occasion. The Chamber also encouraged people to decorate and light up their homes and it was a family tradition to drive the streets of the 'Christmas City.'"

For 15 years (1950/51 - 1966) Bruce published 'North - The Vacation Magazine.' A quarter of a million copies of the full-colour magazine were given to the Chamber free of charge to be used as a direct mail promotion. It was used as guidebook by a variety of outdoor enthusiasts and tourists. It was the start of an overall marketing plan that would become the Near North Travel Area.

Bruce resigned in 1956. One of his fondest memories is raising membership from 89 in 1944 to 588 members at his departure, the largest per capita membership in Canada. "My only regret on leaving the Chamber was I had been unable to reach my objective of 600 members." He will always be remembered for promoting what North Bay had to offer.

Mel

His moustache was ever present and the accomplishments were many through his 9-year career with the Chamber, 1958 to 1966. At the time the Chamber's letterhead motto read: "If the Chamber Doesn't Do It...Who Will?" Mel Mellow did more than his fair share.

He was a member of the Chamber before becoming an employee and remembers helping to start the junior chamber of commerce (Jaycees) in 1951. At the time of his hiring he was selling real estate for Bain and Graham. It was also during Mel's term that the Chamber's office moved to the corner of Fisher and McIntyre Streets. And the Chamber began to staff a summer tourist information booth - built using their own labour - during the first year the bypass was completed. NORAD rock samples were packaged and given out as a giveaway for tourists.

One of his fondest memories was the completion of the Golf St. overpass. The roads and transportation committee worked diligently to make sure the issue remained front and center in community politics. "We discovered Standard Planing Mills was encroaching on an unopened city street with their piles of lumber." Eventually the overpass would use this route to connect North Bay and West Ferris. "It was the wedding ring for amalgamation."

It was during Mel's time that the Chamber endorsed the suggestion that waters from the Harricanaw River be diverted to the Great Lakes system through Lake Nipissing and the French River. The Chamber wondered if such a transportation/irrigation/fresh water project would again rekindle the possibility of a canal scheme of making North Bay a Great Lakes' freighter port. The Harricanaw, emptying into James Bay, would be reversed, diverted and traverse the Arctic/St. Lawrence watersheds, and through an elaborate dam/canal system would eventually join Lake Nipissing.

"The thinking was if it was good for Northern Ontario it was good for North Bay. Duke Kilgour was a big supporter of the project and was instrumental in having the Northeastern Chambers of Commerce support the idea."

What was good for North Bay was the organization of many conventions including the 1959 Canadian Federation of Mayors and Municipalities. "Jack Garland was our M.P. and Prime Minister John Diefenbaker addressed the convention. "A reception was held at the home of Mayor Merle Dickerson and in attendance was movie star Bob Cummings who had been invited by the Chamber through Famous Players Theatres. As Mel recalls "Dief was known for his strict Baptist ways and enjoyed his tomato juice. But I remember him telling a group of us that it was alright to enjoy a little libation." Mel said Jack Garland was "very receptive to Chamber resolutions" and was a man who had "every citizen in mind."

In 1965 the Ontario Chamber of Commerce convention held its second convention in Northern Ontario and North Bay (the first was in 1931). One of the big hospitality events was the docking of the Chief Commanda at Newman Island for a fish fry. "We had to get all the barbecues we could get our hands on and all the pickerel we could buy or catch."

With the Chamber's support the Ontario Trappers Association (OTA) made their fur auction the "wild fur capital of the world," attracting hundreds of international buyers to North Bay. "OTA Manager and Chamber Director Alex Shieff worked diligently to create such a reputation. During the big conventions held by the OTA in North Bay, trappers were transported around town to spend their hard-earned money at North Bay merchants before they returned to the bush."

Mel remembers the issue of four-laning was a constant issue of promotion with the Chamber. "We were always a little fearful of Sudbury and would do anything we could to keep a focus on Highway 11." In the early 1960's and the approaching Expo '67 in Montreal active lobbying revolved around straightening sections of the Trans Canada Highway, especially from North Bay to Mattawa and to Deux Rivieres.

In 1966 the North Bay Parking Authority was formed, an idea the Chamber had "spearheaded through their mercantile committee in 1959." He also remembers the Chamber to be solidly behind the proposed sewage treatment plant and the cleaning up of Chippewa Creek.

The creation of Northeastern University was a major item of business for the Chamber in 1959. Mel recalls Chamber President Herb Brown, asking that the Chamber "get a committee together, including Father Weaver and Jack Trussler." Father Norman Weaver headed Scollard Hall and Mr. Trussler was Superintendent of Schools for the public school board. It was the beginning of a formidable team of "local boosters."

Mel described the "good part of the job," which meant those one-on-one fishing trips with outdoors writers "promoting" the area's favourite spots. "Often we would invite writers from the Globe, Star and Telegram for a weekend of fishing on John Size's boat."

One of Mel's biggest supporters was Nugget editor Mort Fellman. "Anytime I wanted to try something I tried it out on Mort. He was one of the fairest persons I have ever known."

In the Chamber's 1966 annual report Mel reflected upon his past years with the organization. He successfully predicted two areas that the Chamber would begin to tackle. One would be the need to diversify and compete for the tourism and convention dollars. "Conventions continue to be a major source of business revenue and this area has always been able to attract its share." Secondly, Mel saw "the most serious problem facing this Chamber is inadequate financing to meet the demands for publicity and promotional expenses as well as spiralling administrative costs."

And he ended his tenure with some words about "community spirit," a concept Mel still believes in. "More people should share the rich experience of actively participating in the work of the Chamber, if only for the satisfaction and assurance that you are doing your part to help your community flourish. Thus it will become a better place to raise and educate your families."

Chamber of Commerce Secretary-Manager, Mel Mellow (right) with Al Jackson, President in 1958.

Glen

Glen DeVuono started his career with the Chamber on December 1, 1966. He remembers attending the annual meeting the previous month and saying that replacing Mel Mellow meant that he had big shoes to fill. Little did he know that the new job with the Chamber was more than a job, it was a lifestyle.

There have been many changes over the years. The Chamber budget back then was less than $20,000 annually; now it is over $300,000. The staff numbered two; now there are five plus a number of students and part-time people. Despite the changes, much remains the same, according to Glen. "The Chamber still exists to help business succeed and to assist in the development of the community."

It was during his tenure that the Chamber ceased being an "old boys club". Dorothy Venner was the first woman elected to the Board. She chaired the retail committee and had rules that all had to follow, Glen recalls. Her rules: "Meetings will be called only if there is something to discuss. They will begin on time and move along quickly. They will adhere closely with the agenda, to give matters at hand careful consideration. No person shall monopolize the discussion. All extraneous chit chat will be relegated to the end of the meeting for an idea session. To put it briefly, I should like to avoid the futility of sawing sawdust." Glen adds, " it is a shame that these meeting rules are not adopted universally."

Mrs. Venner was soon followed on the Board of Directors by Alice Jones of Fairview Tent and Trailer Park and Mae Beatty of Beatty Printing. In 1977 Daphne Mayne of Mayne Travel Services was elected the first female president. Marie Marchand served in this capacity in 1987 and 1988.

"Partnership" is one of the buzz words of the 90's and Glen states, "an excellent relationship exists between city council, the city administration and the Chamber." This was not always so.

The Chamber, for much of its first 100 years, regarded itself as the official opposition to the city council and often took the Mayor, council and administrators to task. Glen recalls that in 1971 Chamber First Vice President Ed Vitunski claimed in a Nugget story that council was responsible for a multi-million dollar operation, yet ran the city like a junior Red Cross Society. A few years later President George Lowe compared a city council meeting to a popular goofy television show, "The Gong Show".

The first "twinning" on record for Chambers of Commerce in Ontario and Quebec occurred in 1970 when Shawinigan, Quebec and North Bay, Ontario declared themselves twin cities. One of the Shawinigan delegates who visited North Bay that year was a young lawyer and Minister of Indian Affairs and Northern Development, Jean Chretien.

During Glen's time the Chamber has constantly hammered the need for a four-lane Highway 11. In the summer of 1967, the Nugget and the Chamber cooperated in an active campaign for the improvement of the highway north of Gravenhurst. Chamber resolutions sparked support from throughout the north. "The big push indicated the Chamber's unhappiness with the obsolete highway and in time they were successful at least as far as Huntsville."

One of the events that Glen has watched grow is the Chamber's Annual Fall Trade Show. In 1977 the Chamber embarked on a new era as First Vice President George Lowe organized an industry show at Memorial Gardens. This format was soon changed to attract the public to a variety of displays. The weekend event continues to be a major fundraiser for the Chamber. As well, the Ontario North Gift Show was first organized in 1988 by Director Glenn Edmonds and continues to serve the giftware industry of Northern and Central Ontario.

Glen, who in 1992 was presented with a gold Chamber ring in recognition of 25 years of service, has high praise for Chamber volunteers, especially presidents. "It is amazing just how hard Chamber presidents work knowing full well that there is no personal gain for them. The manager and the president work very closely and usually a good relationship develops so it is sad in a way when a new president is elected and the old one retires. But it is this very process that keeps the Chamber a healthy organization, one that has endured for a hundred years", he said.

Glen DeVuono says the economic well being of a community "depends to a large extent upon its citizens supporting local

Front Cover of the Chamber's 1979 annual report, featuring its first home on Main Street, near the ONR's original headquarters. Nipissing Archives/North Bay Area Museum photo.

business." He said this has been emphasized over the years by special "Shop Local" committees set up by the Chamber. The first major campaign was organized during the term of President Harry Hall in 1979. Posters, buttons counter cards, stickers and billboards were some of the tools used by summer students to get this very important message across.

Concerns about the environment were evident as far back as 1969 when the chamber, concerned about the construction of the "super stack" by INCO, were given assurances in writing by the company that "no harm whatsoever would occur to North Bay's environment."

In the 1970's the Chamber mounted a campaign to collect rusting cars and trucks which littered backyards and fields. More than 500 vehicles were collected in a two-year period at no cost to the owners.

The environment committee evolved into a beautification committee which was responsible for constructing North Bay's first downtown pedestrian mall in summer months and for developing parkettes and green areas in the core area. Ken Esselmont was the first chairman while Gerd Schutz was responsible for the mall construction and beautification projects.

The Board/Chamber has always been concerned about the price of gasoline. This is one of North Bay's earliest service stations across the street from Valenti's on Main Street, circa 1930. Nipissing Archives/North Bay Area Museum photo.

Certificates recognizing organizations and people who brought honour and attention to North Bay were presented regularly at Board of Directors meetings starting in 1968. One of the recepients, and a popular one, was an Ontario Provincial Police tracking dog named Cloud. The German Shepherd with a 90-percent record at tracking fugitives was on hand August 14, 1969 to receive his award. Some of the other recipients: author Louise de Kiriline Lawrence, singer Corinne Ayers, Miles for Millions, educator J.W. Trusler, runner, Jackie Dufresne, Bishop Alexander Carter, Santa Claus Fund Chair Art Haley, Mayor Merle Dickerson, Carnival Chair Bryan Manson, golfer Bill Morland, Elks Boys Choir - Arnie Schmidt, pilot Stan Nichols, conservation authority promoter Murray McLean, department of industries chair Curt Johnson, Terry Evans - North Bay Canoe Club and Alex Shieff - Ontario Trappers Association.

Glen may receive an award for his contributions in the workplace, his dedication speaks for itself.

The excellent relationship that exists between the Canadian Forces Base and City of North Bay is due in part to the efforts of military liaison committees established by the Chamber. Pictured here at one of the frequent meetings are, from left, Chamber director Alex Shieff, President Morley Pringle, Group Captain E.C. Likeness, Base Commander, and Secretary-Manager Glen DeVuono.

The Old And The New

The Gateway Heritage Festival holiday weekend of 1986 was a happy day for the North Bay and District Chamber of Commerce. It marked the official opening of the chamber-managed Regional Information Centre and the Dionne Home Museum.

For 42 years, the Board/Chamber was housed in a small, out-of-place, imitation log building at the corner of Main and Regina Streets and rental space at the corner of McIntyre and Fisher Streets. The original building was built by, and on land owned by the Temiskaming and Northern Ontario Railroad. A small, nominal rent fee ($1) was paid by the Board/Chamber on an annual basis. With age the building tilted as did the floors, water pipes continually froze and it was not uncommon to find an employee armed with a hairdryer trying to thaw the pipes. It was, as Glen DuVuono says, "unceremoniously knocked down by Ontario Northland. The elaborate stone chimney was to have been left standing as a permanent memorial but this too, was hauled away by over-zealous workmen." For several years in the 1960's and 1970's the Chamber offices were located at 403 McIntyre St. East and the Main St. location was used only in the summer as an information centre.

The new, $1-million facility located at the corner of Seymour St. and the North Bay bypass was officially opened by Mayor Stan Lawlor and Chamber President Vic Fedeli. Mr. Fedeli said, "We feel that we have a world-class travel centre here and are looking forward to continued success for the chamber for years to come." And success has been with us for 100 years.

Read On...

There are a few books/booklets concerning the history and development of North Bay. These books and other articles/resources related to the North Bay area can be found at the North Bay Public Library, as well as the library at the education centre for Nipissing University and Canadore College.

1909 - Gateway to Silverland, Anson Gard, Emerson Press, Toronto (a book written by a roving American reporter, written for an American audience).

1914 - North Bay 1913/14, North Bay Board of Trade, North Bay (much work done by A.R. Rorabeck, druggist, promotion and marketing of the community, photos are priceless).

1919 - French River Improvement - A Booklet Devoted to Economic Transportation, The Northern Associated Boards of Trade, Strathmore Press, Toronto (a economic look at the viability of the Georgian Bay Ship Canal, heavily sponsored by North Bay Board of Trade).

1925 - Souvenir - Old Home Week, published by committee, North Bay (a look at when North Bay became a city)

1935 - North Bay Old Home Week - Gateway to the Land of Gold, Central Old Home Week Commitee (additional information about the development and history of the city, information on recent birth of Dionne Quintuplets).

1961 - North Bay: Past, Present and Perspective, W.K.P. Kennedy, T.H. Best, Toronto, (good overview of North Bay development, people and events).

1973 - North Bay Hydro 1885-1973, B.M. Graham, T.H. Best Printing, Toronto (history of North Bay Hydro and impact on community).

1975 - Nipissing From Brule to Booth, Murray Leatherdale, North Bay District Chamber of Commerce (a detailed account of the Nipissing Passageway in aboriginal times, the fur trade and early logging era).

1982 - The Best of Hartley Trussler's North Bay, North Bay and District Chamber of Commerce, Hartley Trussler, (reflections of a man who lived much of North Bay's past).

1982 - Gateway City - The North Bay Story, Michael Barnes, North Bay and District Chamber of Commerce (a chronological look at events, chronicled in North Bay Nugget and other sources).

1990 North Words - The Near North's History, Wilston Steer, Detail Printing, North Bay (short stories on the people, places and events of the Near North's heritage).

Other titles that include North Bay in a different historical context or on another other scale of research are the following: Fort Timiskaming and the Fur Trade, Elaine Mitchell, 1977; From Dugout to Diesel, Bessel VandenHazel 1982, The Northern Connection, Ontario Northland since 1902, Robert Surtees, 1992; A Vast and Magnificent Land, An Illustrated History of Northern Ontario, Bicenntennial Project, 1984; North Bay's Fort Chippewa, 1991 and the War Years, C. Gunning.

BOOSTING THE BAY

Highlights of 100 years of the North Bay Board of Trade/District Chamber of Commerce's History

by

Wilston Steer

For the dedicated and capable people who have volunteered their time and abilities to the many concerns of their community.

North Bay
Ontario, Canada

ISBN 0-9694577-2-3

About the Author

Wilston Steer is a teacher and freelance writer, born and raised in North Bay. He is a graduate of Marshall Park Public School and Chippewa Secondary School. He holds degrees and diplomas from McMaster University, Durham College and Nipissing University. His mother and father initiated the Melrose Smoke Shop (Joke Shop) and were members of the Chamber of Commerce. His passion revolves around the outdoors and heritage. He is the author of North Words - Highlights of the Near North's History, The Lake Nipissing Environment Map and Eco-Voyage, a play that helped the North Bay District Ministry of Natural Resources win a national award. Bill is a featured correspondent for the North Bay Nugget and other publications. He has been honoured with "The Great Literary Dinner Party" award for his writing accomplishments and the Dorothy Walford Memorial Award for environmental work.

With his wife Carrie, he lives in the back woods of Mattawan Township, where the wolves are close and others are not. Bill is currently completing a book on native leader - Ted Nolan - 'Healing and Dreaming' to be published by the Union of Ontario Indians.